TO LEARN, TO LEAD ...

To Serve

HERITAGE HALL COOKBOOK

TO LEARN, TO LEAD . . . *To Serve*

Published by Heritage Hall

Copyright © 2008 by
Heritage Hall
1800 NW 122nd Street
Oklahoma City, Oklahoma 73120
405-749-3001
www.heritagehall.com

Cover photograph and chapter opener photographs
    © 2008 by Claire Riggs
Photographs on pages 3, 4, 6 and 8
    © 2007 and 2008 by Claire Riggs and Wes Sharp
Cover concept by Claire Riggs

This cookbook is a collection of favorite recipes, which are not necessarily original recipes.

ISBN: 978-0-9815305-0-5

Edited, Designed, and Produced by

CommunityClassics™

an imprint of

FRP

P. O. Box 305142
Nashville, Tennessee 37230
800-358-0560

Manufactured in the United States of America
First Printing: 2008
4,000 copies

Heritage Hall's Mission Statement

It is our mission to inspire the curiosity TO LEARN, the self-confidence TO LEAD, and the compassion To Serve.

Table of Contents

Letter from the Chairpersons

In May of 2007, the HHSPA board approached us to become the chairpersons of the Heritage Hall cookbook, *To Serve*. The last cookbook created by Heritage Hall was during the school's formative years. The timing was right to produce another one. One would think that this decision would take some time. However, we found that the answer came to us rather quickly. The answer was a resounding "yes!"

Why would this answer come so easily? We teach our children at Heritage Hall to learn, to lead, and to serve. What better way to instill these values? We chose *To Serve*.

The response to the cookbook has been overwhelming. We received more than 2,300 recipes, which were all tested twice. Though we could not choose them all, we want to thank all contributors for their interest in this project. We narrowed it down to the 180 recipes you find in this book. Our hope is that *To Serve* will be a lasting heritage to our school and its families.

We are thankful to so many. The remarkable generosity of our sponsors, the diligence of our chapter chairpersons, the talent and endurance of our test kitchen chefs, and the patience of the staff at Heritage Hall have all made this project possible. We would also like to thank Claire Riggs, photographer and graphic designer, for raising the bar and creating a book that is as beautiful as it is useful. The many sponsors and volunteer hours contributed will make this fund-raiser a culinary and technological success.

The proceeds from this project will directly enhance our children's technology. We look forward to watching our children enjoy the benefits brought about by your support. Thank you so much for your dedication. We have been honored *To Serve*!

Bon appétit!
Janet McLain and Amy Crowley

Committee Members

Appetizers: Christina Mayo

Salads & Vegetables: Jennifer Allen, Cindy Riesen, Tracey Saunders

Brunch & Breads: Crystal Hardberger, Nancy Petersen

Entrées: Kara Brown, Christy Gordon, Patti Lewis

Pasta: Janna Brooks Cole '80

Desserts: Stephanie Collison, Gwen Niemann

Chef Recipes: Kelley Meacham, Denise Remondino

Distribution: Cathy Emerson

Sponsors

Anonymous (2)
Mark and Jennifer Allen
Link and Nicole Barr
Christopher and Julie Bridges
Tony and Sharon Caldwell
Link and Bonnie Clifton
Raymond and Sherry Cohlmia
Steve '78 and Janna Brooks Cole '80
Kevin '80 and Amy Crowley
David and Libby Denner
Everett and Jeanetta Dobson
Stephen and Tina Dobson
Nedra Funk
Robert and Stephanie Gonce
Rick and Carolyn Hansing
Bruce and Tina Farha Harroz '74
Bob and Jennifer Jarman
Joe and Sandra Jarman
George K. Joseph and Pushpa Nambi-Joseph
Lance and Julie Keller
Robert, Patti, Adam and Raylee Lewis
Bill '75 and Terry Mathis
Don and Karen Maxwell
Colby and Christina Mayo
Mrs. R. T. McLain
Scott and Janet McLain
Tim and Liz McLaughlin
Greg and Kelley Meacham
Charles and Kelly Mirabile
David '84 and Kery Mueller
Steven and Stacy Murry
Bob and Denise Remondino
Roberts Building Company
    Bill and Sandy Roberts, Corbyn and Joanna Roberts
Robert '78 and Tracey Saunders
Snoddy Properties
    Jim '75 and Julia Snoddy
Jim and Jenny Turner
Jon and Louise Valuck

To Serve Guide

To Learn: cooking tips, culinary history, and recipe preparation tips

To Lead: pairing of different recipes throughout the cookbook

To Serve: presentation suggestions and variations of the recipe

The Golden Torch Watermark

The recipes that received this marking
are the most outstanding in each section.
They are truly the best of the best.

Appetizers

Appetizers

Crab Empanadas

Crab Artichoke Canapés

Marinated Shrimp

Key West Conch Fritters

Asian Meatballs

Green Chile and Cheese Snacks

Jalapeño Bites

Mushroom Cups

Hot Cheese Olives

Spinach Soufflé Squares

Tomato Bruschetta

Spicy Pretzels

Bread Pot Fondue

Hot Artichoke and Feta Dip

Kalamata Olive Aïoli Spread

Sun-Dried Tomato Dip

Simply Salsa

Cherry Pepper Salsa

Cranberry Salsa

Mango Salsa

Crab Empanadas

1 onion, finely chopped	1 tablespoon rice vinegar
1 tomato, seeded and finely chopped	$1/2$ teaspoon fresh thyme
1 tablespoon butter	Kosher salt to taste
12 ounces lump crab meat	Freshly ground pepper to taste
1 tablespoon chopped flat-leaf parsley	2 refrigerator pie pastries or your own pastry dough
$1/4$ cup drained small capers	1 egg, beaten
	1 tablespoon water

Sauté the onion and tomato in the butter in a large skillet for 5 minutes. Stir in the crab meat, parsley, capers, vinegar, thyme, salt and pepper. Cook for 5 minutes, stirring frequently. Remove from the heat and let cool to room temperature. Roll out the pastries on a lightly floured work surface to $1/8$ inch thick. Cut into $2^{1}/2$-inch rounds with a biscuit cutter. Place 1 teaspoon of the crab mixture onto the center of each pastry round. Moisten the edges of the pastry rounds with ice water and fold over to seal. Press the edges with the tines of a fork to seal. Arrange the empanadas on a lightly buttered baking sheet. Chill until baking time. Mix the egg and water in a bowl. Brush the empanadas with the egg mixture. Bake at 375 degrees for 25 minutes or until light brown. The empanadas may be frozen before baking. Increase the baking time to 30 to 35 minutes if frozen. **Makes 20 to 24.**

Paula Walker

Mother of Mark Walker '71, Lynn Walker Stonecipher '78 and Rob Walker '85
Grandmother of Callahan Walker '17 and Kate Walker '19

Paula was a board member from '84–'85. She was also the Mother's Club President during this time.

Crab Artichoke Canapés

2 tablespoons all-purpose flour
1/8 teaspoon dried thyme
1/8 teaspoon pepper
4 ounces egg substitute
1/4 cup chopped roasted red bell peppers
1 (14-ounce) can artichoke hearts,
drained and chopped
1 (6-ounce) can crab meat, drained
32 won ton wrappers
3 tablespoons grated Parmesan cheese
2 tablespoons chopped chives
1 tablespoon butter, melted

Combine the flour, thyme, pepper and egg substitute in a bowl and mix well. Add the roasted peppers, artichoke hearts and crab meat and mix well. Coat thirty-two miniature muffin cups with nonstick cooking spray. Press one won ton wrapper over the bottom of each muffin cup, allowing the ends to extend above the top of the muffin cup. Spoon the crab meat mixture into the won ton cups. Sprinkle with the cheese and chives. Brush the edges of the won ton wrappers with the melted butter. Bake at 350 degrees for 20 minutes. **Makes 32.**

Janet McLain
Mother of Davis Angel '14 and Grant McLain '20

Marinated Shrimp

1¹/2 pounds medium or large deveined
peeled cooked shrimp
2 tomatoes, finely chopped
1 large avocado, finely chopped
4 to 6 fresh jalapeño chiles, finely chopped
¹/4 cup chopped cilantro
¹/2 cup fresh lime juice
3 tablespoons olive oil
Pepper to taste

Combine the shrimp, tomatoes, avocado, jalapeño chiles, cilantro, lime juice, olive oil and pepper in a bowl and mix well. Chill, covered, for 4 to 8 hours. Serve with tortilla chips. **Serves 10.**

Bonnie Ross
Grandmother of Ross Clifton '12, Camile Clifton '13
and Bella Clifton '15

To Serve: Serve in a large glass candy jar with a
lid. It is always fun to let the guests dip in. You can also place
individual portions in shot glasses.

Key West Conch Fritters

1/2 cup chopped celery
1/2 cup chopped onion
1/4 cup chopped green
bell pepper
1/4 cup chopped red
bell pepper
8 ounces ground conch meat
8 ounces deveined peeled
fresh shrimp, chopped
1 egg
1 egg white
2 tablespoons milk
1 tablespoon white wine
1/2 teaspoon hot red
pepper sauce

1 teaspoon Worcestershire
sauce
6 tablespoons all-purpose flour
1/3 cup Italian-style
bread crumbs
1 teaspoon sugar
1 teaspoon baking powder
1/4 teaspoon salt
1/8 teaspoon cayenne pepper
1/4 teaspoon white pepper
1/4 to 1/2 teaspoon
Italian seasoning
2 tablespoons grated
Parmesan cheese
Peanut oil for deep-frying

Combine the celery, onion, green bell pepper, red bell pepper, conch meat, shrimp, egg, egg white, milk, wine, hot sauce, Worcestershire sauce, flour, bread crumbs, sugar, baking powder, salt, cayenne pepper, white pepper, Italian seasoning and cheese in a bowl and mix until well combined; do not overmix. Chill for 2 hours. Heat peanut oil to 350 degrees in a deep fryer. Drop the conch mixture by tablespoonfuls carefully into the hot oil. Fry in batches until brown. Remove to paper towels to drain. Serve with cocktail sauce. **Makes 40.**

Laurie McCann Hyde
Mother of Jimmy McCann and Margot McCann '87.
Stepmother of Laurie Hyde Moeller '90 and in loving memory
of Jimmy Hyde '88.

To Learn: You may substitute shrimp for the conch to make shrimp fritters, using a total of 1 pound shrimp.

Asian Meatballs

5 pounds lean ground pork
6 (6-ounce) cans water chestnuts,
drained and chopped
3 bunches green onions, chopped
6 eggs, lightly beaten
1/4 cup soy sauce
1/2 teaspoon rosemary, crushed
1 tablespoon salt
Pepper to taste
2 1/2 cups dry bread crumbs
1 cup cornstarch
Vegetable oil or olive oil for frying
1 cup vinegar
2 cups pineapple juice
3/4 cup sugar
2 cups beef consommé
2 tablespoons soy sauce
3 tablespoons chopped crystallized ginger
1/2 cup cornstarch
1 cup water

Mix the pork, water chestnuts and green onions in a bowl. Add the eggs, 1/4 cup soy sauce, the rosemary, salt, pepper and bread crumbs and mix well. Chill until cooking time. Shape the pork mixture into 1-inch balls and coat in 1 cup cornstarch. Heat 1/2 to 1 inch oil in a heavy skillet. Add the meatballs in batches and fry until brown. Remove to paper towels to drain. Mix the vinegar, pineapple juice, sugar, consommé, 2 tablespoons soy sauce, the ginger, 1/2 cup cornstarch and the water in a large saucepan. Cook until thickened, stirring frequently. Add the meatballs and cook until heated through, stirring occasionally. This recipe may be halved. The meatballs may be frozen after cooking and before adding to the sauce. **Serves 25 to 30.**

Jeri L. Richardson in loving memory of Shirley Hamilton
Mother of Avery L. Richardson '19 and Rylee A. Richardson '22

Green Chile and Cheese Snacks

1/2 cup (2 ounces) shredded
sharp Cheddar cheese
3 ounces cream
cheese, softened
2 tablespoons chopped
black olives

1 (4-ounce) can chopped
green chiles
1 teaspoon dried onion flakes
5 drops of hot red pepper sauce
1 (8-count) can refrigerator
crescent rolls

Mix the Cheddar cheese, cream cheese, olives, green chiles, onion flakes and hot sauce in a bowl. Unroll the crescent dough on a work surface. Separate the dough into four rectangles, pressing the perforations to seal. Spread one-fourth of the cheese mixture over each rectangle. Roll up from the long side and cut each roll into ten slices. Arrange the slices on a well greased baking sheet. Bake at 400 degrees for 12 to 15 minutes or until golden brown. Serve hot. These were first made in 1981! They are a long-time family favorite. **Makes 40.**

Marlene Magrini-Greyson
Mother of David Greyson '09

Jalapeño Bites

6 fresh or pickled jalapeño chiles, cut into halves and seeded
3 ounces cream cheese, softened
4 slices bacon, cut into thirds

Stuff each jalapeño chile half with equal amounts of the cream cheese. Wrap one bacon piece around each stuffed jalapeño chile and secure with a wooden pick. Arrange, stuffed side up, in a shallow baking pan. Bake at 350 degrees until the bacon is cooked through. Remove to paper towels to drain. Serve hot or at room temperature. **Makes 12.**

Lynne Walker Stonecipher '78

To Learn: The heat of the jalapeño varies with how many seeds are left inside. Wearing rubber gloves while seeding the jalapeño chiles is advised.

Mushroom Cups

2 loaves very thin sandwich bread
1/4 cup chopped celery
1/4 cup chopped onion
1/4 cup (1/2 stick) butter
2 tablespoons all-purpose flour
1 cup finely chopped mushrooms
2 tablespoons grated Parmesan cheese
1/2 teaspoon salt
1/8 teaspoon (or more) cayenne pepper
1 teaspoon lemon juice
1 cup heavy cream
1 tablespoon chopped parsley

Microwave the bread slices for 10 seconds to warm slightly. Cut each slice into rounds using a wine glass or biscuit cutter. Press the bread rounds over the bottom of nonstick miniature muffin cups. Bake at 375 degrees for 7 to 8 minutes or until the bread cups are toasted; maintain the oven temperature. Sauté the celery and onion in the butter in a skillet until tender. Stir in the flour. Add the mushrooms and sauté until the mushrooms are tender. Stir in the cheese, salt, cayenne pepper, lemon juice, cream and parsley. Cook until thickened, stirring frequently. Spoon the mushroom mixture into the bread cups. Bake for 5 to 10 minutes. **Makes 40.**

Stefanie Dolese
Mother of Stefan Dolese '14, Liesl Dolese '15
and Renie Dolese '15

To Serve: Chopped fresh parsley or chives can be added before serving to add a little color.

Hot Cheese Olives

1/2 cup (1 stick) butter, softened
8 ounces shredded sharp Cheddar cheese,
at room temperature
1 cup all-purpose flour
1 teaspoon salt
1/4 teaspoon cayenne pepper
70 small pimento-stuffed green olives

Combine the butter, cheese, flour, salt and cayenne pepper in a bowl and mix well. Wrap a marble-size piece of dough around each olive. Arrange the olives on a nonstick baking sheet. Bake at 350 degrees until golden brown and crisp. Serve hot. **Makes 70.**

Evaline Thompson
Grandmother of Lance Cook '98, Trent Cook '01, Kylee Keller '16,
Chandler Keller '18 and Gray Keller '24

To Learn: You may double the recipe and
freate the unbaked olive balls. Thaw before baking. These are
perfect for a large cocktail party or to use at a later time.

Spinach Soufflé Squares

1 cup minced onion
1/2 cup (1 stick) butter
2 (10-ounce) packages frozen chopped spinach,
cooked and drained
2 cups herb-seasoned stuffing mix
1/2 cup (2 ounces) grated Parmesan cheese
1/4 cup (1/2 stick) butter, melted
5 eggs, beaten
1/2 teaspoon pepper
Garlic salt or garlic powder to taste

Sauté the onion in 1/2 cup butter in a skillet until tender. Remove the onion and butter to a bowl. Add the spinach, stuffing mix, cheese, 1/4 cup melted butter, eggs, pepper and garlic salt and mix well. Chill for 3 hours or longer. Spread the spinach mixture into a 9×11-inch baking pan. Bake at 350 degrees for 45 minutes or until set. Cut into small squares and keep warm in a chafing dish. You may also shape the mixture into balls and bake for 20 minutes. **Makes 36 to 48.**

Patricia Meyers
Grandmother of Mary-Alice Brown '07, Jesse Brown '10
and Reilly Brown '14

Beth Wells
Mother of Courtney Wells '99 and Brenna Wells '02

Tomato Bruschetta

4 large vine-ripened tomatoes
1 cup (4 ounces) finely chopped fresh
mozzarella cheese
1/3 cup chopped fresh basil
3 garlic cloves, minced
2 tablespoons chopped fresh parsley
2 tablespoons olive oil
1/2 teaspoon salt
1/2 teaspoon pepper
3 garlic cloves
1 loaf crusty Italian bread,
cut into 1/2-inch slices

Cut the tomatoes horizontally into halves and squeeze out the seeds. Chop the tomatoes finely and remove to a colander; drain for 30 minutes. Remove the tomatoes to a bowl. Add the cheese, basil, minced garlic, parsley, olive oil, salt and pepper and mix well. Crush the three garlic cloves slightly with the side of a large knife and remove the peels. Rub the garlic over the bread slices. Discard the garlic. Toast the bread on both sides under a broiler or on a grill. **Serves 8.**

Linda Bell
Great-aunt of Britni Griffin '12 and Chandler Griffin '16

*To Serve: Remove the tomato mixture to a small
serving bowl and center on a platter. Surround
with the bread slices and allow guests to serve themselves.
You may also spread the tomato mixture over the bread
slices and arrange on a decorative platter.*

Spicy Pretzels

1 teaspoon cayenne pepper
1/2 teaspoon lemon pepper
1 1/2 teaspoons garlic salt
1 envelope original ranch salad dressing mix
1/2 to 3/4 cup vegetable oil
1 (24-ounce) package small pretzel twists

Whisk the cayenne pepper, lemon pepper, garlic salt, salad dressing mix and oil in a bowl. Pour over the pretzels in a sealable plastic bag. Seal the bag and shake or turn to mix. Shake or turn the bag occasionally for 2 hours. **Makes 1 1/2 pounds.**

Stacy Stevens Townsdin '80 and
Ron Townsdin '79

Sheila Campbell
Mother of Scott Campbell '08

To Serve: Place in a decorative bag for a hostess gift.
These are impossible to quit eating.

Bread Pot Fondue

1 (10-inch) round loaf Hawaiian-style bread
2 tablespoons olive oil
1 tablespoon butter, melted
1 cup (4 ounces) shredded Cheddar cheese
1 cup (4 ounces) shredded Monterey Jack cheese
6 ounces cream cheese, softened
1 1/2 cups sour cream
1 cup diced ham
1/2 cup chopped green onions
1 (4-ounce) can chopped green chiles, drained
2 teaspoons Worcestershire sauce

Slice off the top of the bread and reserve. Hollow out the bread, leaving a 1/2-inch shell. Cut the removed bread into 1-inch cubes. Combine the bread cubes, olive oil and melted butter in a bowl and toss to coat. Spread the bread cubes on a baking sheet. Bake at 350 degrees for 10 minutes or until golden brown; maintain the oven temperature. Combine the Cheddar cheese, Monterey Jack cheese, cream cheese and sour cream in a bowl and mix well. Stir in the ham, green onions, green chiles and Worcestershire sauce. Spoon the mixture into the bread shell and replace the top of the bread. Wrap the bread loaf in foil and place on a baking sheet. Bake for 1 hour and 10 minutes or until heated through. Serve with the toasted bread cubes, celery sticks or crackers. **Serves 8 to 10.**

Bonnie McAffrey
Great-aunt of Delaney Mayo '16,
Dylan Mayo '20 and Daylee Mayo '23

To Learn: A recipe for a sauce made from Pramnos wine,
grated goat cheese and white flour appears in Scroll 11
of Homer's Iliad and has been cited as the earliest record of fondue.

Hot Artichoke and Feta Dip

8 ounces light cream
cheese, softened
1 (14-ounce) can artichoke
hearts, drained and chopped
2 garlic cloves, minced

1/2 cup (2-ounces) shredded
Parmesan cheese
1 (3-ounce) package regular
or reduced-fat crumbled
feta cheese

Combine the cream cheese, artichoke hearts, garlic and Parmesan cheese in a bowl and mix well. Spread in a 9-inch pie plate or 3-cup ovenproof serving dish. Top with the feta cheese. Bake at 350 degrees for 20 to 25 minutes. Serve hot with crackers. **Serves 10 to 12.**

Tina Farha Harroz '74
Mother of Briana Harroz '13 and Cole Harroz '16

To Serve: Add a little cayenne pepper or Tabasco sauce for a spicier version. A touch of curry powder also adds an interesting flavor!

Kalamata Olive Aïoli Spread

4 ounces kalamata olives,
pitted and well drained
1 ounce Parmesan cheese,
coarsely grated

4 (or more) garlic cloves
1 ounce fresh basil leaves
2 cups mayonnaise
Salt and pepper to taste

Combine the olives, cheese, garlic and basil in a food processor and process until the mixture begins to thicken. Add the mayonnaise and process for 2 minutes. Season with salt and pepper. Remove to a serving bowl. Chill, covered, until cold. Serve with baguette slices. **Serves 12.**

Dashea Beesing Gelnar '81
Mother of Colton Gelnar '15 and Leighton Gelnar '15

To Serve: Place the aïoli in a cut crystal bowl. Whole kalamata olives on top are the perfect garnish.

Sun-Dried Tomato Dip

2 tablespoons to 1/2 cup
fresh basil
10 sun-dried tomatoes,
rehydrated and chopped
1 cup part-skim ricotta cheese
2 tablespoons
nonfat mayonnaise
1/4 cup plain nonfat yogurt
2 tablespoons low-fat
cream cheese
2 teaspoons (or more)
minced garlic
2 teaspoons olive oil

Combine the basil, tomatoes, ricotta cheese, mayonnaise, yogurt, cream cheese, garlic and olive oil in a food processor and process until smooth. Remove to a serving bowl. Chill, covered, to blend flavors; the garlic will intensify. Serve with pita chips, bagel chips or crackers. **Serves 6 to 8.**

Jules Hefley Deer
Aunt of Hunter Wade '14 and Zane Wade '18

To Learn: This is low-fat for those watching their waistline!

Simply Salsa

3 or 4 green onions
1 garlic clove
1 jalapeño chile
1 (28-ounce) can whole tomatoes, drained
2 sprigs of cilantro
Salt and pepper to taste

Process the green onions, garlic and jalapeño chile in a food processor until chopped. Add the tomatoes and process to reach the desired consistency. Add the cilantro and process briefly. Season with salt and pepper. Pour into a serving bowl. Simply fast, easy and tasty! **Serves 8 to 10.**

Nancy Karum, Lower School Secretary

Cherry Pepper Salsa

2 (14-ounce) cans stewed tomatoes
2 tomatoes, chopped
12 bottled mild cherry peppers (about 1 jar)
6 to 8 green onions, chopped
2 (4-ounce) cans chopped black olives, drained
$2^1/4$ cups mild picante sauce
1 (3-ounce) bottle Louisiana hot sauce
2 teaspoons garlic salt
1 teaspoon pepper
Dash of vinegar or cherry pepper juice

Combine the stewed tomatoes, tomatoes, cherry peppers, green onions, olives, picante sauce, hot sauce, garlic salt, pepper and vinegar in a mixing bowl. Beat to mix well. **Serves 16 to 20.**

Cheryl Barnes, Lower School Secretary

To Serve: You may add more hot sauce if you like a kick. You must hurry to get a bite as the bowl will soon be empty.

Cranberry Salsa

12 ounces fresh cranberries
1/4 cup chopped cilantro
2 jalapeño chiles

1 bunch green onions
1 tablespoon vegetable oil
3/4 cup sugar

Combine the cranberries, cilantro, jalapeño chiles and green onions in a food processor. Pulse until finely chopped but not puréed. Remove to a bowl and fold in the oil and sugar. Chill until cold. Serve over a block of cream cheese with crackers. **Serves 8 to 10.**

Sheryl Shaw
Mother of Kaleb Robertson '14 and Kate Shaw '19

To Serve: The salsa is perfect for Christmas parties. You can also serve it with chips or on Kam's Kookery Fish Tacos (page 155).

Mango Salsa

2 to 3 large ripe mangoes, peeled, pitted and diced
1 medium or 2 small jalapeño chiles, seeded and minced
3/4 cup chopped red bell pepper

2 tablespoons lime juice
1/2 teaspoon salt
1/4 teaspoon cayenne pepper
1/8 teaspoon (or more) cumin
3 tablespoons chopped cilantro, or to taste

Combine the mangoes, jalapeño chiles, bell pepper, lime juice, salt, cayenne pepper and cumin in a bowl and mix well. Chill for 3 hours or longer. Add the cilantro and toss to combine. Chill for 1 hour or longer. This recipe will keep, covered, for several days in the refrigerator. Serve with tortilla chips. **Serves 8.**

Gladys Collison
Grandmother of Sydney Collison '14, Macy Collison '16
and Tori Collison '19

To Serve: This salsa is great served over grilled chicken or fish.

Salads & Vegetables

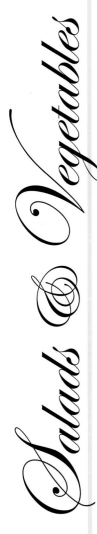

Salads & Vegetables

Baby Spinach Salad with Pears and Gorgonzola

Champagne Salad with Pear and Goat Cheese Tartlets

Delicious Fall Salad

Jackson Salad

Blue Cheese Caesar Salad

Company Salad

Strawberry Romaine Salad

Sweet and Savory Salad

Chinese Chicken Salad

The Cellar Chicken Salad

Chicken Salad with Homemade Mayonnaise

Asparagus Tomato Salad

Roasted Pepper and Tomato Salad

Green Beans au Gratin

Roasted Cauliflower with Prosciutto

Oven-Roasted Sweet Potatoes and Acorn Squash

Spinach-Stuffed Tomatoes

Baby Spinach Salad with Pears and Gorgonzola

6 ounces baby spinach
6 ounces crumbled Gorgonzola cheese
5 green onions, thinly sliced
1/2 cup sliced almonds
1 pear, chopped
1/4 cup sugar
1/4 cup vegetable oil
1/4 cup apple cider vinegar
Salt and pepper to taste

Combine the spinach, cheese, green onions, almonds and pear in a serving bowl and toss to combine. Combine the sugar, oil, vinegar, salt and pepper in a jar with a tight-fitting lid and shake until the sugar is dissolved. Add the desired amount of dressing to the salad and toss to coat. Let stand for 5 minutes before serving. **Serves 6 to 8.**

Megan Cramer Christensen '90

To Learn: A melon baller or metal 1/2-teaspoon measuring spoon is perfect to carve out the core of a pear quickly and easily.

Champagne Salad with Pear and Goat Cheese Tartlets

Vinaigrette	Salad
1/4 cup olive oil	1 1/2 cups pecans or
1/4 cup champagne vinegar	walnuts, chopped
2 tablespoons honey	3/4 cup sugar
Dijon mustard	2 refrigerator pie pastries
1 tablespoon honey	8 ounces goat cheese,
3/4 teaspoon sea salt	at room temperature
1/2 teaspoon freshly	2 tablespoons honey
ground pepper	1 teaspoon dried thyme
	5 ounces mixed baby lettuce
	5 ounces arugula
	1/2 cup sweetened
	dried cranberries

For the vinaigrette, whisk the olive oil, vinegar, honey Dijon mustard, honey, salt and pepper in a bowl. Chill for 30 minutes.

For the salad, mix the pecans and sugar in a saucepan. Cook over medium heat for 10 minutes or until the sugar is melted and golden brown, stirring constantly. Watch carefully so that the sugar doesn't burn. Spread the pecans over waxed paper to cool. Unroll the pie pastries on a work surface. Cut into rounds using a biscuit cutter or wine glass. Fit the pastry rounds over the bottom of greased miniature muffin cups, shaping to form shells. Bake at 375 degrees for 8 to 10 minutes. Remove to a wire rack to cool. Combine the cheese, honey and thyme in a bowl and mix well. Spoon into the baked tartlet shells. Combine the lettuce and arugula in a serving bowl and toss to combine. Sprinkle with the pecans and cranberries. Arrange the tartlets around the edge of the salad. Drizzle with the vinaigrette and serve. **Serves 12.**

Christina Mayo
Mother of Delaney Mayo '16, Dylan Mayo '20 and
Daylee Mayo '23

Delicious Fall Salad

1 head romaine, torn
into bite-size pieces
1 head iceberg lettuce, torn into bite-size pieces
1 cup (4 ounces) shredded mozzarella cheese
1 cup (4 ounces) shredded Parmesan cheese
1 cup sweetened dried cranberries
8 ounces bacon, crisp-cooked and crumbled
1 cup toasted slivered almonds
1/2 cup red wine vinegar
1 cup sugar
1 teaspoon salt
2 teaspoons prepared mustard
1/4 cup finely chopped red onion
1 cup vegetable oil

Combine the romaine, iceberg lettuce, mozzarella cheese, Parmesan cheese, cranberries, bacon and almonds in a serving bowl and toss to combine. Whisk the vinegar, sugar, salt, mustard and onion in a bowl. Whisk in the oil. Add the desired amount of dressing to the salad and toss to coat. **Serves 12.**

Deborah Brannon
Mother of Alexis Brannon '11

To Serve: This is beautiful for a Thanksgiving buffet.
The cranberries add a festive holiday touch.

Jackson Salad

2 heads romaine, torn into bite-size pieces
1 (8-ounce) can hearts of palm, drained and
cut into bite-size pieces
1 (14-ounce) can artichoke hearts, drained and
cut into bite-size pieces
8 ounces bacon, crisp-cooked and crumbled
4 ounces blue cheese
1 cup (or less) vegetable oil
1/4 cup minced onion
1/4 to 1/2 cup vinegar
2 teaspoons dry mustard
1/2 teaspoon sugar
1/2 teaspoon salt
1/4 teaspoon pepper

Combine the lettuce, hearts of palm, artichoke hearts, bacon and cheese in a serving bowl and toss to combine. Whisk the oil, onion, vinegar, mustard, sugar, salt and pepper in a bowl. Add to the salad and toss to coat. **Serves 8.**

Jennifer Allen
Mother of Matt Allen '04, Claire Allen '06 and
Katherine Allen '15

Blue Cheese Caesar Salad

1 large head romaine
1/2 cup vegetable oil
1/2 teaspoon salt
1/4 teaspoon pepper
1/2 garlic clove, pressed
1/2 cup (2 ounces) grated Parmesan cheese
1/2 cup (2 ounces) blue cheese, crumbled
1/4 cup fresh lemon juice
1 tablespoon Worcestershire sauce
1 cup croutons

Rinse the lettuce and wrap in paper towels. Chill for 2 hours. Combine the oil, salt, pepper, garlic, Parmesan cheese, blue cheese, lemon juice and Worcestershire sauce in a jar with a tight-fitting lid and shake well. Chill for 2 hours or longer. Tear the lettuce into bite-size pieces into a serving bowl. Add the dressing and toss to coat. Add the croutons and toss to combine. You may quadruple the salad dressing ingredients and store, covered, in the refrigerator for up to 10 days. **Serves 8.**

Margaret Ringwald
Mother of Jeff Ringwald '94 and Lisa Ringwald '97

To Learn: The traditional Caesar salad
was credited to Caesar Cardini who ran restaurants
in Tijuana, Mexico, from 1920–1940.

Company Salad

1 head romaine, torn into
bite-size pieces
1 head green leaf lettuce, torn into
bite-size pieces
1 head red leaf lettuce, torn into
bite-size pieces
1 (15-ounce) jar mangoes, drained and chopped
1 red onion, chopped
1 (15-ounce) can Shoe Peg corn, drained
3 ounces can smoked almonds, chopped
1 red bell pepper, chopped
1 yellow bell pepper, chopped
4 ounces crumbled blue cheese
1/4 cup salad toppings
1/2 cup olive oil
1/2 cup vegetable oil
1/3 cup balsamic vinegar
1 teaspoon Dijon mustard
1/2 teaspoon honey, or to taste

Combine the romaine, green leaf lettuce, red leaf lettuce, mangoes, onion, corn, almonds, red bell pepper, yellow bell pepper, cheese and salad toppings in a serving bowl and toss to combine. Whisk the olive oil, vegetable oil, vinegar, Dijon mustard and honey in a bowl. Add to the salad and toss to coat. **Serves 12.**

Timberly Eckelmann
Mother of Susi Eckelmann '08

To Lead: Perfect for a large crowd served with *Green Hills Brisket (page 91)* or *Welker Brothers' Tailgate Barbecue (page 90).*

Strawberry Romaine Salad

$1/2$ cup almonds
$1/4$ cup sugar
$3/4$ cup sugar
$1/2$ cup red wine vinegar
1 cup vegetable oil
2 garlic cloves, minced
$1/2$ teaspoon salt
$1/2$ teaspoon paprika
$1/4$ teaspoon white pepper
1 large head romaine, rinsed and
torn into bite-size pieces
1 head Boston lettuce, rinsed and
torn into bite-size pieces
1 pint strawberries, sliced
1 cup (4 ounces) shredded Pepper Jack cheese

Combine the almonds and $1/4$ cup sugar in a skillet. Cook over medium heat until the sugar is dissolved and the almonds are golden brown, stirring constantly. Spread the mixture over foil and break apart when cool. Combine $3/4$ cup sugar, the vinegar, oil, garlic, salt, paprika and pepper in a jar with a tight-fitting lid and shake well. Combine the romaine, Boston lettuce, strawberries, cheese and almonds in a serving bowl and toss to combine. Add the desired amount of dressing and toss to coat. Serve immediately. **Serves 8 to 10.**

Kara Brown
Mother of Callan Brown '06 and Travis Brown '08

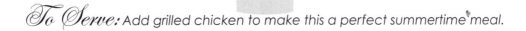

To Serve: Add grilled chicken to make this a perfect summertime meal.

37

Sweet and Savory Salad

1/3 cup sugar
1 teaspoon salt
1 teaspoon dry mustard
1 teaspoon celery seeds
1 teaspoon paprika
1 teaspoon finely chopped green onions
1/2 cup red wine vinegar
1 cup canola oil
3 garlic cloves, minced
3 cups green leaf lettuce
2 cups red leaf lettuce
1 (11-ounce) can mandarin oranges, drained
6 ounces almonds, toasted
2 avocados, sliced
8 ounces sliced mushrooms

Whisk the sugar, salt, mustard, celery seeds, paprika, green onions, vinegar, canola oil and garlic in a bowl. Pour over green leaf lettuce, red leaf lettuce, mandarin oranges, toasted almonds, sliced avocado and mushrooms in a large bowl and toss to combine. **Serves 8.**

Mary Nelson
Aunt of Meg Jarman '12 and Jennings Jarman '15

Chinese Chicken Salad

1/2 (14-ounce) package rice sticks
Vegetable oil for frying
3 chicken breasts, cooked, boned and
cut into bite-size pieces
1 head napa cabbage, shredded
3 to 6 green onions, chopped
1/2 cup sesame seeds, toasted
3 tablespoons sugar
1/4 cup white vinegar
1 teaspoon salt
1/2 teaspoon pepper
1/2 cup vegetable oil

Fry the rice sticks in hot oil in a heavy saucepan until curled but not brown. Remove with a slotted spoon to paper towels to drain. Combine the chicken, cabbage, green onions, sesame seeds and rice sticks in a serving bowl. Cook the sugar, vinegar, salt and pepper in a saucepan over low heat until the sugar is dissolved, stirring occasionally. Remove from the heat and let cool. Whisk in 1/2 cup oil. Pour over the cabbage mixture and toss to coat. Serve immediately. **Serves 8.**

Amy Crowley
Mother of Blake Crowley '14 and Paige Crowley '16

To Learn: Rice sticks can be found in the Asian
section of your grocery store.

The Cellar Chicken Salad

1 1/2 cups mayonnaise
1 teaspoon curry powder
1 tablespoon soy sauce
1 tablespoon lemon juice
3 pounds chicken pieces, cooked, skinned,
boned and coarsely chopped
2 cups chopped celery
1 pound seedless grapes, cut into halves
1 (10-ounce) can water chestnuts,
drained and sliced
1 1/2 cups slivered almonds, toasted
Lettuce leaves
1 cup canned pineapple chunks (optional)
Avocado slices (optional)

Combine the mayonnaise, curry powder, soy sauce and lemon juice in a large bowl and mix well. Fold in the chicken, celery, grapes, water chestnuts and almonds. Chill, covered, for 8 to 10 hours. Serve on lettuce leaves and top with the pineapple and avocado. **Serves 8.**

Susan Berney
Aunt of Ellen Berney, Middle School Art Teacher

Janie Stewart
Mother of Sandra Stewart Brooks '80, Michael Stewart '81,
Jeffrey Stewart '84 and David Stewart '88
Grandmother of Ashley Brooks '07, Amy Brooks '10
and Anna Brooks '13

Chicken Salad with Homemade Mayonnaise

Homemade Mayonnaise
2 eggs
4 cups vegetable oil
3 garlic cloves, pressed
Juice of 1 large lemon
2 teaspoons salt
1 tablespoon paprika

Chicken Salad
8 chicken breasts, cooked, boned and cut into bite-size pieces

Italian salad dressing
1 cup chopped celery
1 cup toasted pecans, chopped
1 (3-ounce) jar capers, drained and rinsed, or
   1 cup seedless grapes, cut into halves
1 cup Homemade Mayonnaise, or to taste

For the mayonnaise, beat the eggs at medium speed in a mixing bowl until frothy. Add the oil in a slow stream, beating constantly. Beat until thick. Add the garlic, lemon juice, salt and paprika and beat well. Store in an airtight container in the refrigerator until ready to use. If you are concerned about using raw eggs, use eggs pasteurized in their shells, or use equivalent amounts of pasteurized egg substitute.

For the chicken salad, combine the chicken and enough salad dressing to moisten in a bowl; toss to coat. Chill, covered, for 8 to 10 hours. Add the celery, pecans and capers or grapes and toss to combine. Add the Homemade Mayonnaise and mix well. **Serves 8.**

Sandra Jarman
Grandmother of Davis Angel '14, Grant McLain '20,
Meg Jarman '12 and Jennings Jarman '15

To Learn: The most important part of making the mayonnaise is to add the oil slowly.

Asparagus Tomato Salad

3 cups water
1 pound asparagus spears, trimmed and
cut into 1-inch pieces
1 pint cherry tomatoes, cut into quarters
1/2 cup sliced green onions
3 tablespoons drained green capers
2 garlic cloves, minced
3 tablespoons olive oil
1 tablespoon fresh lemon juice
41/2 teaspoons red wine vinegar
Kosher salt and pepper to taste

Bring the water to a boil in a saucepan. Add the asparagus and cook for 2 to 3 minutes or until tender-crisp. Plunge into ice water and drain. Remove to a serving bowl. Add the tomatoes, green onions, capers and garlic and toss to combine. Whisk the olive oil, lemon juice and vinegar in a bowl. Add to the salad and toss to coat. Season with salt and pepper. **Serves 4 to 6.**

Sherry Blanton
Mother of Jack Blanton '10 and Bailey Blanton '15

To Learn: Plunging green vegetables in ice water is important after cooking. This process enhances the bright green color and the vegetables won't lose their natural crunch!

Roasted Pepper and Tomato Salad

4 large red bell peppers
8 ounces fresh mozzarella cheese,
cut into 1/2-inch cubes
1 pint cherry tomatoes or grape tomatoes,
cut into halves
3 tablespoons olive oil
2 tablespoons balsamic vinegar
2 tablespoons fresh lemon juice
1/4 cup chopped basil
2 tablespoons chopped mint
Sea salt and pepper to taste

Core the bell peppers and cut into quarters. Arrange, cut side down, on a foil-lined baking sheet. Place under the broiler until slightly blackened. Remove the peppers to a sealable plastic bag and seal the bag. Let stand for 15 minutes. Remove the blackened skin and cut the peppers into strips. Combine the pepper strips, cheese and tomatoes in a serving bowl. Whisk the olive oil, vinegar, lemon juice, basil, mint, salt and pepper in a bowl. Add to the tomato mixture and toss to coat. **Serves 8.**

Christina Mayo
Mother of Delaney Mayo '16, Dylan Mayo '20 and
Daylee Mayo '23

To Serve: Use red, yellow and green bell peppers
for a more colorful presentation.

Green Beans au Gratin

2 cups sliced mushrooms
2 tablespoons minced onion
1/4 cup slivered almonds
1/2 cup (1 stick) butter
1/3 cup all-purpose flour
1/2 teaspoon dry mustard
Salt and pepper to taste
2 cups milk
3/4 cup (3 ounces) shredded Swiss cheese
1 tablespoon lemon juice
1/8 teaspoon Tabasco sauce
3 (14-ounce) cans green beans, drained
1/4 cup almonds
1 tablespoon butter

Sauté the mushrooms, onion and 1/4 cup slivered almonds in 1/2 cup butter in skillet until the mushrooms are tender. Stir in the flour, mustard, salt and pepper. Cook for 1 to 2 minutes, stirring constantly. Stir in the milk and cheese. Cook until thick, stirring constantly. Add the lemon juice, Tabasco sauce and beans and mix well. Spoon into a 2-quart baking dish. Cook 1/4 cup almonds in 1 tablespoon butter in a skillet until the almonds are toasted, stirring frequently. Sprinkle the almonds over the bean mixture. Bake at 350 degrees for 15 to 20 minutes. **Serves 6 to 8.**

Joan White
Mother of Stephen White '78 and Courtney White Sherman '87

To Lead: *This is not your traditional green bean casserole.*
The Swiss cheese and unexpected heat make this a unique dish.
Great served with any of our beef or chicken dishes.

Roasted Cauliflower with Prosciutto

1 head cauliflower, cut into florets
2 to 4 ounces thickly sliced prosciutto, cut into 1/4-inch cubes
1/2 cup pitted dates, chopped
2 tablespoons extra-virgin olive oil
1/2 teaspoon salt
1/4 teaspoon red pepper flakes
1 tablespoon chopped parsley

Mix the first six ingredients in a bowl. Spread in a 10×15-inch baking pan. Roast in the top half of the oven at 375 degrees for 30 to 40 minutes or until the cauliflower is tender and light brown, stirring occasionally. Remove to a serving platter or bowl and sprinkle with the parsley. **Serves 6 to 8.**

Diane Surtees
Mother of Bailey Surtees '13 and Monica Surtees '15

To Serve: You may substitute bacon, but prosciutto gives the BEST flavor! If using bacon, partially cook it before adding it to the recipe.

Oven-Roasted Sweet Potatoes and Acorn Squash

3 sweet potatoes, peeled and cut into cubes
1 large acorn squash, seeded and cut into half-moon slices
1 large shallot, chopped
1 sweet onion, sliced
1 red onion, sliced
1/3 cup olive oil
Minced garlic to taste
Salt and pepper to taste

Combine the ingredients in a large sealable plastic bag. Seal and turn the bag to coat. Remove the vegetables to a shallow baking pan. Roast at 425 degrees for 40 minutes. **Serves 6.**

Tracey Saunders
Mother of Trent Saunders '13 and Sayde Saunders '17

Spinach-Stuffed Tomatoes

6 firm tomatoes
Salt and pepper to taste
6 slices bacon
2 (10-ounce) packages frozen spinach,
cooked, drained and squeezed dry
2 garlic cloves, minced
2 eggs, beaten
2/3 cup plus 2 tablespoons grated Parmesan cheese
1/2 cup heavy cream or evaporated milk

Cut 1/2 inch off the top of the tomatoes. Scoop out the seeds and pulp to form a shell and discard the seeds and pulp. Sprinkle the inside of the tomatoes lightly with salt and pepper. Invert the tomato shells onto paper towels to drain for 30 minutes. Cook the bacon in a skillet until crisp. Remove with a slotted spoon to paper towels to drain; crumble the bacon. Reserve 1/4 cup of the bacon drippings in the skillet and discard the remaining drippings. Add the spinach to the reserved bacon drippings and sauté until heated through. Add the garlic and sauté for 2 minutes. Remove from the heat. Beat the eggs, 2/3 cup of the cheese and the cream in a bowl. Season with salt and pepper. Add the spinach mixture and two-thirds of the bacon and mix well. Sprinkle 1 teaspoon of the remaining cheese inside each tomato shell. Fill the tomato shells with equal amounts of the spinach mixture. Arrange the tomatoes, stuffed side up, in a lightly oiled baking dish. Bake at 325 degrees for 30 minutes; do not overcook. Sprinkle with the remaining crumbled bacon and serve. **Serves 6.**

Linda Bell
Great-aunt of Britni Griffin '12 and Chandler Griffin '16

To Lead: Great served with Standing Rib Roast with
Roasted Potatoes and Horseradish Sauce (page 86).

Brunch & Breads

Brunch & Breads

Dutch Crab Salad Sandwiches

Green Chile Chorizo Breakfast Quiche

Blue Cheese and Artichoke Grits

Blueberry Smoothie

Caramel French Toast Casserole

The Best Coffee Bundt Cake

Blue Ribbon Cinnamon Rolls

Blueberry Muffins

Angel Family Gingerbread Muffins

Pumpkin Chocolate Chip Muffins

Apricot Pumpkin Bread

Cranberry Banana Bread

Spicy Pineapple Zucchini Bread

Tasty Greek Bread

New Faculty Dinner Bread

Veggie Corn Bread

Mom's Biscuits

Melt-In-Your-Mouth Overnight Rolls

Dutch Crab Salad Sandwiches

6 ounces cream cheese, softened
4 slices bacon, crisp-cooked
and crumbled
1 teaspoon lemon juice
1 teaspoon
Worcestershire sauce
Dash of Tabasco sauce
1 tablespoon chopped onion
1 (6-ounce) can crab meat, drained
4 large croissants, sliced in half horizontally
4 slices sharp Cheddar cheese
4 slices tomato

Combine the cream cheese, bacon, lemon juice, Worcestershire sauce, Tabasco sauce, onion and crab meat in a bowl and mix well. Spread the mixture equally over the bottom halves of the croissants. Top each with a slice of Cheddar cheese and a slice of tomato. Replace the tops of the croissants and serve. **Serves 4.**

Judy Clay
Former 6th- and 7th-grade math teacher

To Serve: We serve this for Sunday brunch with fresh fruit and asparagus.

Green Chile Chorizo Breakfast Quiche

1 pound chorizo sausage, casings removed
2 or 3 (4-ounce) cans whole green chiles, drained
4 ounces shredded Monterey Jack cheese
5 eggs
1/2 cup milk
1/4 teaspoon pepper

Brown the sausage in a skillet, stirring until crumbly. Remove the sausage to paper towels to drain. Cut each chile halfway through lengthwise and lay the chiles flat. Coat a 9-inch pie plate with nonstick cooking spray. Arrange the chiles over the bottom and up the side of the prepared pie plate to form the crust. Sprinkle the sausage and cheese evenly over the chiles. Beat the eggs lightly in a bowl. Beat in the milk and pepper. Pour the egg mixture into the pie plate. Bake at 350 degrees for 30 minutes or until a knife inserted halfway between the center and edge comes out clean. Let stand for 10 minutes before cutting. **Serves 6 to 8.**

Livy Evans Huelskamp '90
Mother of Kaitlyn Huelskamp '14 and Trey Huelskamp '18

To Learn: In an effort to be more health conscious,
this recipe has been made with "soyrizo," reduced-fat cheese, and
egg substitute. We couldn't tell the difference!

Blue Cheese and Artichoke Grits

3 cups milk
1 garlic clove, crushed
1 teaspoon salt
1 cup quick-cooking grits
1 cup (4 ounces) crumbled blue cheese
5$^1/_3$ tablespoons butter, cut into cubes
$^1/_2$ cup whipping cream
3 eggs, lightly beaten
1 (8-ounce) can artichoke hearts,
drained and chopped
2 teaspoons basil
$^1/_4$ teaspoon pepper

Bring the milk, garlic and salt to a boil in a saucepan. Stir in the grits gradually and reduce the heat. Simmer, covered, for 10 minutes, stirring occasionally. Whisk in the cheese and butter and cook until melted, whisking constantly. Whisk in the cream, eggs, artichoke hearts, basil and pepper. Pour into a lightly greased 1$^1/_2$-quart soufflé dish. Bake at 325 degrees for 1 hour and 10 minutes; the center may be soft. **Serves 8.**

DeDe Jarman
Great-aunt of Meg Jarman '12, Jennings Jarman '15,
Davis Angel '14 and Grant McLain '20

To Serve: To serve as an appetizer, bake in a 9×12-inch baking dish for 50 minutes or until set. Cut into squares when slightly cool.

Blueberry Smoothie

Light vanilla soy milk
6 ounces vanilla or berry low-fat yogurt
Pomegranate juice
Frozen blueberries
1 banana (optional)

Pour a couple of splashes of soy milk into a blender. Add the yogurt and a splash of pomegranate juice. Process until well blended. Add a few handfuls of blueberries and the banana. Process at high speed until puréed. Add additional soy milk or pomegranate juice if the mixture is too thick, or additional blueberries if too thin. **Serves 2.**

Melissa Gutwald
Mother of Matthew Gutwald '16

To Learn: Blueberries and pomegranates are loaded with antioxidants. *It is a great way to get kids to have a healthy start to their day.*

Caramel French Toast Casserole

1 cup packed brown sugar
1/2 cup (1 stick) butter
2 tablespoons corn syrup
10 to 12 slices bread
1 teaspoon cinnamon
1/4 cup granulated sugar
6 eggs
1 1/2 cups milk
1/2 teaspoon vanilla extract
1/2 teaspoon cinnamon

Cook the brown sugar, butter and corn syrup in a skillet until boiling, stirring constantly. Pour evenly into a greased 9×13-inch baking dish. Arrange five to six slices bread over the syrup mixture. Mix 1 teaspoon cinnamon and the granulated sugar in a bowl. Sprinkle one-half of the cinnamon-sugar over the bread in the baking dish. Arrange the remaining slices bread over the top and sprinkle with the remaining cinnamon-sugar. Mix the eggs, milk, vanilla and 1/2 teaspoon cinnamon in a bowl. Pour evenly over the bread. Chill for 8 to 10 hours. Remove from the refrigerator 30 minutes before baking. Bake at 350 degrees for 30 minutes.
Serves 12

Sandra Hardberger
Grandmother of Kate Hardberger '16 and Max Harberger '19

*To Serve: Great with syrup! It is beautiful if you
turn the square caramel side up and serve with sliced strawberries
and a sprinkle of confectioners' sugar.*

The Best Coffee Bundt Cake

Cake
1/2 cup (1 stick) butter, softened
1/2 cup chopped pecans
1 (2-layer) package yellow cake mix
1 (4-ounce) package vanilla instant pudding mix
3/4 cup water
3/4 cup vegetable oil
4 eggs
1 1/2 teaspoons vanilla extract
1 1/2 teaspoons butter flavoring
1/4 cup sugar
1/3 cup chopped pecans
2 teaspoons cinnamon

Glaze
1 1/2 cups confectioners' sugar
3 tablespoons milk
1/2 teaspoon vanilla extract
1/2 teaspoon butter flavoring

For the cake, coat the inside of a bundt pan with the butter and sprinkle with 1/2 cup pecans. Beat the cake mix, pudding mix, water and oil in a mixing bowl. Add the eggs one at a time, beating well after each addition. Beat for 6 minutes. Beat in the vanilla and butter flavoring. Combine sugar, 1/3 cup pecans and the cinnamon in a bowl and mix well. Spoon the batter into the bundt pan alternately with the cinnamon mixture, beginning and ending with the batter. Bake at 350 degrees for 40 to 60 minutes or until the cake tests done. Cool in the pan for 10 minutes. Invert onto a serving plate.

For the glaze, combine the confectioners' sugar, milk, vanilla and butter flavoring in a bowl and stir until smooth. Drizzle over the bundt cake. **Serves 12 to 16.**

Darlene Miller
Grandmother of Madison Mueller '12 and Caroline Mueller '15

To Serve: Using a decorative bundt pan adds to the presentation. The drizzle is most easily accomplished by dipping a spoon into the glaze and letting it trickle off.

Blue Ribbon Cinnamon Rolls

1 cup granulated sugar
1 teaspoon salt
3 envelopes dry yeast
8 to 9 cups bread flour
2 cups milk
1 cup (2 sticks) butter
2 eggs
1/4 cup (1/2 stick) butter, melted
1/2 cup packed brown sugar

1/2 cup pecans
1/2 cup raisins
1 teaspoon cinnamon
2 cups confectioners' sugar
  (optional)
3 tablespoons water (optional)
1/2 teaspoon vanilla extract
  (optional)

Mix the granulated sugar, salt, yeast and 2 cups of the flour in a large mixing bowl. Heat the milk and 1 cup butter in a saucepan until very warm; the butter does not have to melt completely. Beat the milk mixture gradually into the dry ingredients at low speed. Increase the speed to medium and beat for 2 minutes. Beat in the eggs and 2 cups of the remaining flour. Beat for 2 minutes, scraping down the side of the bowl occasionally. Stir in enough of the remaining flour to make about 4 cups soft dough. Knead the dough on a floured surface for 10 minutes or until smooth and elastic. Shape the dough into a ball and place in a greased bowl, turning to coat the surface. Let rise, covered, in a warm place for 1 hour or until doubled in bulk. Punch the dough down. Divide the dough into halves. Roll each half into a 12×18-inch rectangle on a floured surface. Brush with the melted butter. Mix the brown sugar, pecans, raisins and cinnamon in a bowl. Sprinkle the cinnamon mixture evenly over each rectangle. Roll up from the long side and pinch the seam to seal. Cut one roll, seam side down, into 1-inch slices. Arrange the slices, cut side down, in a well greased 9×13-inch baking pan. Repeat with the remaining roll and arrange in a second baking pan. Let rise, covered, in a warm place for 40 minutes or until doubled in bulk. Bake at 400 degrees for 25 minutes. Cool in the pan until warm. Remove to a serving plate.

Combine the confectioners' sugar, water and vanilla in a bowl and stir until smooth. Drizzle over the rolls. **Serves 30.**

Katherine Lagaly
Aunt of Avery Niemann '15 and Ashton Niemann '18

Blueberry Muffins

4 cups all-purpose flour
2 cups sugar
2 tablespoons baking powder
2 teaspoons salt
4 eggs
1/2 cup vegetable oil

1/2 cup (1 stick) butter, melted
1 1/2 cups milk
2 teaspoons vanilla extract
16 ounces frozen or fresh
   blueberries
Sugar for sprinkling

Sift the flour, sugar, baking powder and salt into a bowl. Make a well in the center and add the eggs, oil, butter, milk and vanilla to the well. Stir gently just until the liquid is absorbed. Fold in the blueberries. Fill paper-lined muffin cups three-fourths full. Sprinkle the tops of the muffins with sugar. Bake at 350 degrees for 30 to 40 minutes or until the centers of the muffins are firm. Remove to a wire rack to cool. **Serves 24 to 30.**

Racinda Ross
Mother of Brynn Ross '05 and Brogan Ross '07

To Learn: Freezing the blueberries keeps them from sinking in the batter.

Angel Family Gingerbread Muffins

2 1/2 cups all-purpose flour
2 1/2 teaspoons baking soda
1 teaspoon salt
1 teaspoon cinnamon
1 teaspoon ginger

1 cup (2 sticks) butter
1 cup molasses
1 cup boiling water
2 eggs, beaten

Sift the flour, baking soda, salt, cinnamon and ginger together. Combine the butter, molasses and water in a bowl and mix well. Add the dry ingredients and mix well. Stir in the eggs. Bake immediately or store the batter, covered, in the refrigerator for up to 5 days. Fill greased muffin cups two-thirds full. Bake at 350 degrees for 30 to 40 minutes or until the muffins test done. Serve warm with butter. **Serves 12.**

Mary Jo Schneider
Grandmother of Davis Angel '14

Pumpkin Chocolate Chip Muffins

1 2/3 cups all-purpose flour
3/4 cup sugar
1 teaspoon baking soda
1 teaspoon cinnamon
1/4 teaspoon baking powder
1/4 teaspoon salt
1/2 cup (3 ounces) miniature chocolate chips
2 eggs
3/4 cup canned pumpkin
1/2 cup (1 stick) margarine, melted
1/4 cup milk
1/2 teaspoon vanilla extract

Mix the flour, sugar, baking soda, cinnamon, baking powder and salt in a bowl. Stir in the chocolate chips. Whisk the eggs, pumpkin, margarine, milk and vanilla in a bowl. Add to the dry ingredients and stir just until mixed. Spoon the batter into greased or paper-lined muffin cups. Bake at 350 degrees for 20 to 25 minutes. Cool in the pan for 5 minutes. Remove to a wire rack to cool slightly and serve warm. **Serves 12.**

Sheryl Shaw
Mother of Kaleb Robertson '14 and Kate Shaw '19

To Serve: These are great any time of the year,
but especially during the Thanksgiving holiday. You will be very
thankful for the amazing taste of chocolate and pumpkin.

Apricot Pumpkin Bread

2¹/4 cups all-purpose flour
1¹/2 teaspoons baking soda
1¹/2 teaspoons baking powder
3/4 teaspoon each cinnamon,
    nutmeg and salt
1¹/2 cups canned pumpkin
1 cup sugar

1 cup vegetable oil
3 eggs
1 (4-ounce) package vanilla
    instant pudding mix
1¹/2 cups chopped
    dried apricots
1¹/2 cups chopped walnuts

Sift the first six ingredients together. Combine the pumpkin, sugar, oil and eggs in a bowl and mix well. Stir in the dry ingredients. Fold in the pudding mix. Stir in the apricots and walnuts. Pour into two greased loaf pans. Bake at 350 degrees for 1 hour or until a wooden pick inserted in the center comes out clean. Cool in the pans for 10 minutes. Remove to a wire rack to cool completely. **Serves 24.**

Arlene McIntyre
Great-aunt of Kate Hardberger '16 and Max Hardberger '19

Cranberry Banana Bread

2 cups all-purpose flour
1¹/2 teaspoons baking powder
1 teaspoon salt
1/2 teaspoon baking soda
1/4 cup (1/2 stick) butter,
    softened
1¹/4 cups sugar

1 egg, beaten
2/3 cup mashed banana
1¹/4 cups fresh or frozen
    cranberries, coarsely
    chopped
1/2 cup chopped pecans
    or walnuts

Sift the first four ingredients together. Beat the butter and sugar in a bowl. Add the egg and beat until smooth. Add the dry ingredients and stir just until mixed. Fold in the banana, cranberries and pecans. Spoon into a nonstick 5x9-inch loaf pan. Bake at 350 degrees for 65 to 70 minutes or until a wooden pick inserted near the center comes out clean. Cool in the pan for 10 minutes. Remove to a wire rack to cool completely. **Serves 12.**

Debbi Dudley
Mother of Matt Dale '01 and Alex Dudley '10

Spicy Pineapple Zucchini Bread

3 cups all-purpose flour
2 teaspoons baking soda
1 teaspoon salt
1/2 teaspoon baking powder
1 1/2 teaspoons cinnamon
3/4 teaspoon nutmeg
1 cup walnuts, finely chopped (optional)
1 cup currants, finely chopped (optional)
3 eggs
1 cup vegetable oil
2 cups sugar
2 teaspoons vanilla extract
2 cups coarsely shredded zucchini
1 (8-ounce) can crushed pineapple, drained

Mix the flour, baking soda, salt, baking powder, cinnamon, nutmeg, walnuts and currants in a bowl. Beat the eggs with a rotary beater in a bowl. Add the oil, sugar and vanilla and beat until foamy. Stir in the zucchini and pineapple. Add the dry ingredients and stir just until mixed. Spoon into two greased and floured 5×9-inch loaf pans. Bake at 350 degrees for 1 hour or until wooden picks inserted near the centers come out clean. Cool in the pans for 10 minutes. Remove to a wire rack to cool completely. **Serves 24.**

Cindy Coletti
Grandmother of Lola Coletti '21 and Isabelle Coletti '22

To Learn: The easiest way to shred zucchini
is to use the large holes of a box grater. Dry any excess moisture
from the zucchini with paper towels.

Tasty Greek Bread

3 envelopes fast-rising dry yeast
2 cups warm water
8 1/2 cups all-purpose flour
3/4 cup sugar
1 tablespoon salt
1/2 teaspoon cinnamon
4 egg yolks
2 egg whites
1/4 cup orange juice
1 tablespoon olive oil
3 tablespoons brandy
1/2 cup (1 stick) butter, softened
1 egg yolk, beaten
Sesame seeds (optional)

Dissolve the yeast in the warm water in a bowl; set aside. Mix the flour, sugar, salt and cinnamon in a large bowl. Add the yeast mixture, four egg yolks, the egg whites, orange juice, olive oil, brandy and butter and mix with clean hands or beat with an electric mixer. Add additional flour if the mixture is sticky. Cover with a towel and let rise in a warm place for 2 hours. Knead on a floured surface and divide the dough into halves. Place each half in a greased loaf pan or greased 9-inch baking pan. Cover and let rise in a warm place for 1 hour. Brush the tops of the bread with one egg yolk and sprinkle with sesame seeds. Bake at 350 degrees for 5 minutes. Reduce the oven temperature to 300 degrees and bake for 25 minutes longer. **Makes 2 loaves.**

Mary Pappas
Grandmother of Daniel Pappas '08

To Learn: To revive a loaf of stale bread,
just place the bread in a brown paper sack. Sprinkle the sack
with water. Bake at 350 degrees for 5 minutes.

New Faculty Dinner Bread

1/2 cup (1 stick) margarine, softened
1/2 cup mayonnaise
(do not use salad dressing)
1 (4-ounce) can chopped black olives, drained
6 (or more) scallions, finely chopped
1/2 to 1 teaspoon cayenne pepper
2 cups (8 ounces) shredded
mozzarella cheese
1 large baguette or
loaf Italian bread, cut lengthwise

Combine the margarine, mayonnaise, olives, scallions and cayenne pepper in a bowl and mix well. Stir in the cheese. Spread over the cut sides of the bread. Arrange the bread, cut side up, on a baking sheet. Bake at 350 degrees for 15 minutes or until toasty. Slice and serve. **Serves 12.**

Julie Bramble
Upper School Teacher and
wife of Guy Bramble, Headmaster of Heritage Hall
Mother of Kristen Bramble '99 and Jamie Bramble '05

Veggie Corn Bread

2 (8-ounce) packages corn bread mix
4 eggs
10 ounces cottage cheese
1 (10-ounce) package frozen chopped
broccoli, thawed
1 onion, chopped
1 red bell pepper, chopped
3/4 cup (1 1/2 sticks) butter, melted

Combine the corn bread mix, eggs, cottage cheese, broccoli, onion, bell pepper and butter in a bowl and mix well. Pour into a nonstick 9×13-inch baking pan. Bake at 350 degrees for 40 minutes. This bread freezes well. You may substitute one 16-ounce can black-eyed peas, drained, for the broccoli for a New Year's bread. **Serves 24.**

Judy Savage
Mother of Lane Savage '01

To Lead: The test kitchen loved it with the
Famous Tenderloin Chili (page 92).

Mom's Biscuits

2 2/3 cups milk
2 envelopes dry yeast
2/3 cup sugar
2/3 cup shortening
3 cups all-purpose flour
4 1/3 cups all-purpose flour
1 1/3 teaspoons salt
4 teaspoons baking powder
2/3 teaspoon baking soda

Heat the milk in a saucepan until hot. Remove from the heat and let cool until warm. Mix the warm milk and yeast in a large bowl. Add the sugar, shortening and 3 cups flour and mix well. Let rise in a warm place for 2 hours. Stir in 4 1/3 cups flour, the salt, baking powder and baking soda. Knead on a floured surface four or five times. Roll out to 3/4 to 1 inch thick. Cut into rounds using a biscuit cutter or upside down juice glass. Arrange the biscuits on a greased baking sheet. Bake at 400 degrees for 10 to 12 minutes or until golden brown. Serve hot with butter, honey, jam or apple butter. **Makes 24 biscuits.**

In memory of Barbara Julian
Grandmother of Delaney Mayo '16, Dylan Mayo '20 and
Daylee Mayo '23

To Learn: You may double the recipe.
Cut out the dough and freeze. Just pop in the oven
on a busy night!

Melt-In-Your-Mouth Overnight Rolls

1 envelope dry yeast
1 teaspoon sugar
1/2 cup warm water
1 egg, beaten
1 1/2 teaspoons salt
1/2 cup sugar
1/2 cup vegetable oil
2 cups hot milk
6 cups all-purpose flour
Melted butter

Dissolve the yeast and 1 teaspoon sugar in the water in a bowl. Beat the egg, salt and 1/2 cup sugar in a large mixing bowl. Add the oil, milk and yeast mixture and beat well. Add the flour 1 cup at a time, beating well after each addition. Chill, covered, for 8 to 10 hours. Roll out the dough on a floured surface. Cut into rounds with a biscuit cutter. Brush each round with melted butter and fold in half. Arrange the rolls in a greased baking dish. Brush the tops with melted butter. Let rise in a warm place for 2 hours. Bake at 400 degrees for 12 to 15 minutes or until golden brown. **Makes 48 rolls.**

Sandra Jarman
Grandmother of Davis Angel '14, Grant McLain '20,
Meg Jarman '12 and Jennings Jarman '15

To Learn: These rolls can be perfected by even the most novice bread bakers!

Pasta

White Lasagna

Pretty Penne Florentine

Asian Pork Tenderloin with Noodles

Beef Rigatoni

The Fergusons' Spaghetti

Spaghetti Bolognese

Baked Chicken Spaghetti

Chicken Piccata Pasta

Chicken Marsala Penne

Mediterranean Shrimp Pasta

Angel Hair Pasta with Eggplant

Penne à la Vodka

Italian Pasta Salad

Greek Pasta Salad

Orzo Salad with Roasted Vegetables

Spinach, Feta and Garbanzo Bean Pasta Salad

Never-Fail Noodles

White Lasagna

12 cups chicken broth
2 large pinches of saffron
16 ounces lasagna noodles
12 ounces mushrooms, sliced
1 cup chopped yellow onion
1/2 cup chopped celery
3 garlic cloves, minced
2 tablespoons olive oil
1 pound ground veal
1 pound bulk pork sausage
2 teaspoons dried basil
2 teaspoons dried oregano
1 teaspoon Italian seasoning
1/2 teaspoon salt
1 cup half-and-half
6 ounces cream cheese

1/2 cup dry white wine
1/2 cup (2 ounces) shredded
  Cheddar cheese
1 1/2 cups (6 ounces) shredded
  Gouda cheese
Cayenne pepper to taste
12 ounces small curd
  cottage cheese
1 egg, beaten
3 tablespoons chopped
  fresh parsley
9 ounces fresh baby spinach
6 to 8 cups (24 to 32 ounces)
  shredded mozzarella cheese
Paprika to taste

Bring the broth, a small amount of water and the saffron to a boil in a large saucepan. Remove from the heat and let stand for a few minutes. Return to the heat and bring to a boil. Add the noodles and cook until al dente; drain. Sauté the mushrooms, onion, celery and garlic in the olive oil until the vegetables are tender. Remove from the heat and set aside. Brown the veal and sausage in a skillet, stirring until crumbly; drain. Add the mushroom mixture. Stir in the basil, oregano, Italian seasoning, salt, half-and-half and cream cheese. Cook until the cream cheese is melted, stirring constantly. Add the wine, Cheddar cheese and Gouda cheese. Cook until the cheese is melted, stirring constantly. Season with cayenne pepper. Combine the cottage cheese, egg and parsley in a bowl and mix well. Layer the noodles, meat mixture, cottage cheese mixture, spinach and mozzarella cheese one-fourth at a time in 9×13-inch baking pan, ending with a thick layer of mozzarella cheese. Sprinkle with paprika. Bake at 350 degrees for 40 minutes. Let stand for 10 minutes before serving. **Serves 12.**

Janet McLain
Mother of Davis Angel '14 and Grant McLain '20

To Learn: The saffron-infused noodles make this a special dish. *Infusion means to steep an aromatic ingredient in hot liquid.*

Pretty Penne Florentine

1 pound Italian sausage or
turkey sausage, casings removed
3 garlic cloves, minced
2 cups drained crushed tomatoes
1/2 cup chicken broth
1/2 cup white wine
4 handfuls of spinach leaves
1 teaspoon dried basil or
1 tablespoon chopped fresh basil
1/2 cup (2 ounces) shredded mozzarella cheese
1/4 cup (1 ounce) grated Parmesan cheese
Salt and pepper to taste
Tabasco sauce to taste
12 ounces penne, cooked and drained

Brown the sausage in a skillet, stirring until crumbly; drain. Add the garlic and sauté for 1 minute. Stir in the tomatoes, broth and wine. Cook for 10 minutes. Turn off the heat and stir in the spinach and basil. Let stand, covered, for 5 minutes. Stir in the mozzarella cheese, Parmesan cheese, salt, pepper and Tabasco sauce. Stir in the pasta and serve. **Serves 6 to 8.**

Diane Surtees
Mother of Bailey Surtees '13 and Monica Surtees '15

*To Serve: This goes together in about 30 minutes.
It is pretty and delicious enough to serve to company! To prepare
ahead of time, just keep the noodles and sauce
separate and add the spinach and cheese when you reheat.*

Asian Pork Tenderloin with Noodles

1 cup olive oil
3/4 cup red wine vinegar
1 teaspoon sesame oil
1 teaspoon red chile oil
1 tablespoon Tabasco sauce
Juice of 1 lime
1/2 cup regular or light soy sauce
2 bunches green onions, chopped
1/4 cup chopped cilantro
1 tablespoon (or less) hot red pepper flakes
1 teaspoon white pepper
3 garlic cloves, minced
2 (1-pound) pork tenderloins
8 ounces spaghetti, cooked and drained

Whisk the olive oil, vinegar, sesame oil, chile oil, Tabasco sauce, lime juice, soy sauce, green onions, cilantro, red pepper flakes, white pepper and garlic in a large shallow dish. Add the pork and turn to coat. Marinate in the refrigerator for 2 hours, turning occasionally. Remove the pork and pour the marinade into a saucepan. Bring the marinade to a boil and boil for 5 minutes. Cook the pork on a preheated grill until cooked through. Combine the pasta with the hot marinade in a bowl and toss to coat. Slice the pork and serve with the pasta on the side. **Serves 6.**

DeDe Jarman
Great-aunt of Meg Jarman '12, Jennings Jarman '15,
Davis Angel '14 and Grant McLain '20

To Serve: You may also marinate chicken breasts
instead of pork tenderloins.

Beef Rigatoni

1 pound lean ground beef
1 1/2 teaspoons butter
1 1/2 cups chopped yellow onions
2 garlic cloves, chopped
3/4 cup parsley, chopped
1 teaspoon Italian seasoning
2 (8-ounce) cans tomato sauce
1 tablespoon prepared basil pesto
1 (8-ounce) can mushrooms
1 cup burgundy
Salt and pepper to taste
12 ounces rigatoni, cooked and drained well
Grated Parmesan cheese

Brown the ground beef in the butter in a skillet, stirring until crumbly; drain. Add the onions and garlic and sauté until the onions are tender. Stir in the parsley, Italian seasoning, tomato sauce, pesto, mushrooms, wine, salt and pepper. Simmer, uncovered, for 2 hours, stirring occasionally. Adjust the seasonings to taste. Add the pasta and toss to combine. Sprinkle with cheese and serve with additional cheese on the side. **Serves 6 to 8.**

Denise Remondino
Mother of Molly Remondino '14 and Annie Remondino '18

To Serve: You may use ground venison for a more full-bodied flavor.

The Fergusons' Spaghetti

3 pounds ground beef
2 large onions, chopped
6 (6-ounce) cans tomato paste
6 to 8 garlic cloves, minced
1 cup parsley, chopped
1 cup chopped celery with leaves
1 cup chopped green bell pepper
2 1/2 tablespoons salt
2 tablespoons sugar
3 tablespoons chili powder
2 bay leaves
1 teaspoon dried oregano
8 ounces mushrooms, sliced
1/2 cup (1 stick) butter
Hot cooked spaghetti

Brown the ground beef with the onions in a heated large saucepan, stirring until the ground beef is crumbly and the onions are translucent; drain. Reduce the heat and stir in the tomato paste, garlic, parsley, celery, bell pepper, salt, sugar, chili powder, bay leaves, oregano and mushrooms. Simmer for 2 hours, stirring occasionally. Add water if the sauce seems too thick. Adjust the seasonings to taste. Remove and discard the bay leaves. Add the butter and cook until the butter is melted, stirring constantly. Combine the pasta with a few ladles of the sauce in a large saucepan and cook briefly over high heat, tossing constantly. Serve the remaining sauce over the pasta. **Serves 12 to 14.**

Jay Ferguson '96,
Director of Performing Arts at Heritage Hall

Kristen Bramble '99

Spaghetti Bolognese

2 tablespoons olive oil
4 ounces bacon, diced
1 1/2 cups chopped yellow onions
1 cup diced carrots
1 cup diced celery
1 heaping tablespoon minced garlic
1 1/2 teaspoons salt
1 teaspoon pepper
2 bay leaves
1 teaspoon dried thyme
1/2 teaspoon dried oregano
1 teaspoon cinnamon
1 teaspoon nutmeg
1 pound ground veal or ground beef

8 ounces bulk pork sausage
2 tablespoons tomato paste
1 cup dry red wine
1 (28-ounce) can good-quality crushed tomatoes
1 (28-ounce) can tomato sauce
1 cup beef broth
2 teaspoons sugar
1/4 cup heavy cream
2 tablespoons unsalted butter
3 tablespoons chopped fresh parsley
16 ounces spaghetti, cooked and drained
Freshly grated Parmesan cheese

Heat the olive oil in a large saucepan over medium-high heat. Add the bacon and sauté for 4 to 5 minutes or until the bacon is crisp and the drippings are rendered. Add the onions, carrots and celery and sauté for 4 to 5 minutes or until the vegetables are tender. Add the garlic, salt, pepper, bay leaves, thyme, oregano, cinnamon and nutmeg and sauté for 30 seconds. Add the ground veal and sausage and cook for 5 minutes or until the meat is crumbly and no longer pink, stirring constantly. Add the tomato paste and cook for 1 to 2 minutes, stirring constantly. Add the wine and cook for 2 minutes or until the liquid is reduce by half, scraping up any brown bits from the bottom of the pan. Stir in the tomatoes, tomato sauce, broth and sugar and bring to a boil. Reduce the heat to medium-low. Simmer for 45 to 60 minutes or until the sauce has thickened, stirring occasionally. Stir in the cream, butter and parsley and cook for 2 minutes. Remove and discard the bay leaves and adjust the seasonings to taste. Combine the sauce and hot pasta in a bowl and toss to combine. Sprinkle with cheese and serve. This sauce freezes well. **Serves 8 to 10.**

Julie Stewart
Mother of Lizzie Stewart '15 and Luke Stewart '18

Baked Chicken Spaghetti

1 chicken
Salt and pepper to taste
3/4 cup chopped onion
1/4 cup chopped green bell pepper
1 garlic clove, crushed
1 (2-ounce) can sliced mushrooms, drained
51/3 tablespoons butter
1/4 cup all-purpose flour
1 cup canned diced tomatoes
1/4 teaspoon sugar
4 ounces American cheese or Cheddar cheese, shredded
~~8 ounces~~ spaghetti, cooked and drained
1/2 cup buttered bread crumbs
Paprika to taste

[handwritten: Whole box]

Simmer the chicken in a large saucepan of seasoned water until cooked through. Remove the chicken to a work surface and reserve the stock. Chop the chicken, discarding the skin and bones. Sauté the onion, bell pepper, garlic and mushrooms in the butter in a hot skillet until the vegetables are tender. Stir in the flour. Cook for 1 to 2 minutes, stirring constantly. Stir in 2 cups of the reserved stock, salt and pepper. Cook until thickened, stirring constantly. Stir in the tomatoes, sugar, cheese and cooked chicken. Cook until the cheese is melted, stirring frequently. Alternate layers of the pasta with the chicken mixture in a greased 9×13-inch baking pan. Top with the bread crumbs and sprinkle with paprika. Bake at 375 degrees for 25 to 30 minutes. **Serves 8.**

Wanda Brundrett (Mrs. Leyton)
Grandmother of Blake Crowley '14 and Paige Crowley '16

To Serve: This is a comfort food for the entire family.
Serve with our Sweet and Savory Salad (page 38) and
Melt-In-Your-Mouth Overnight Rolls (page 64).

Chicken Piccata Pasta

2 tablespoons olive oil
1 1/3 pounds boneless chicken breasts,
cut into 1-inch pieces
Salt and pepper to taste
Additional olive oil
1 tablespoon butter
4 garlic cloves, minced
2 shallots, finely chopped
2 tablespoons all-purpose flour
1/2 cup dry white wine
Juice of 1 lemon
1 cup chicken broth
3 tablespoons capers, drained and rinsed
1/2 cup parsley, chopped
1 1/2 teaspoons butter
16 ounces penne, cooked,
drained and kept warm

Heat 2 tablespoons olive oil in a large skillet and add the chicken. Season with salt and pepper and sauté until the chicken is golden brown and cooked through. Remove the chicken with a slotted spoon to a platter. Add a small amount of olive oil and 1 tablespoon butter to the skillet. Add the garlic and shallots and sauté for 3 minutes. Stir in the flour. Cook for 2 minutes, stirring constantly. Whisk in the wine and cook for 1 minute. Whisk in the lemon juice and broth. Stir in the capers and parsley. Add 1 1/2 teaspoons butter and the chicken. Cook until heated through, stirring occasionally. Add the pasta and toss to combine. Garnish with chopped chives and grated Parmesan cheese and serve. **Serves 4.**

Janna Brooks Cole '80
Mother of Jordan Cole '08, Elaine Cole '10 and Carter Cole '20

To Lead: This is a wonderful summer dish served with the Asparagus Tomato Salad (page 42) and a loaf of crispy French bread.

Chicken Marsala Penne

4 boneless skinless chicken breasts
Salt and pepper to taste
Paprika to taste
$1/2$ cup all-purpose flour
1 tablespoon cornstarch
3 bouillon cubes, crushed
2 tablespoons olive oil
1 tablespoon butter
2 or 3 garlic cloves, chopped
$1/4$ cup sliced scallions
8 ounces mushrooms, sliced
$1/2$ cup marsala
1 cup hot chicken broth
1 tablespoon butter, softened
1 tablespoon all-purpose flour
$1/2$ cup half-and-half
16 ounces penne, cooked, drained and kept warm

Cut the chicken into medallions and season with salt, pepper and paprika. Mix $1/2$ cup flour, the cornstarch and bouillon cubes in a sealable plastic bag. Add the chicken and turn the bag to coat. Remove the chicken, shaking off any excess flour mixture. Heat the olive oil and 1 tablespoon butter in a skillet until hot. Add the chicken. Cook the chicken for 2 to 3 minutes per side or until golden brown and cooked through. Remove the chicken with tongs to a platter and keep warm. Add the garlic, scallions and mushrooms to the skillet. Sauté for 3 minutes. Stir in the wine and broth. Mix 1 tablespoon butter and 1 tablespoon flour in a bowl. Add to the skillet. Cook until the mixture thickens slightly, stirring constantly. Add the chicken and half-and-half. Cook until heated through, stirring frequently. Spoon over the pasta and serve immediately. **Serves 4.**

Sydney Graves Carey '79

To Learn: Marsala is a wine produced in the region
surrounding the Italian city of Marsala in Sicily.

Mediterranean Shrimp Pasta

3 garlic cloves, minced
4 green onions, sliced
2 tablespoons olive oil
1 1/2 (7-ounce) jars marinated
artichoke hearts
5 Roma tomatoes, chopped
1 cup mushrooms, sliced
1/4 cup dry white wine
2 teaspoons Italian seasoning
1/4 teaspoon dried rosemary, crushed
1/4 teaspoon salt
1/4 teaspoon pepper
1 pound medium fresh shrimp, peeled
8 ounces linguini, cooked,
drained and kept warm

Sauté the garlic and green onions in the olive oil in a skillet over medium heat until tender. Stir in the undrained artichoke hearts, tomatoes, mushrooms, wine, Italian seasoning, rosemary, salt and pepper. Bring to a boil and reduce the heat. Simmer for 5 minutes, stirring occasionally. Stir in the shrimp and cook for 3 minutes or until the shrimp turn pink. Serve over the pasta and garnish with freshly grated Parmesan cheese. **Serves 4 to 6.**

Kery Mueller
Mother of Madison Mueller '12 and Caroline Mueller '15

Angel Hair Pasta with Eggplant

8 ounces angel hair pasta
Salt to taste
2 tablespoons olive oil
1 large eggplant, peeled and
cut into 1-inch cubes
1 tablespoon olive oil
4 garlic cloves, chopped
6 tomatoes, diced
1 small jar spaghetti sauce
2 tablespoons sugar
Pepper to taste
Hot red pepper flakes to taste
1/2-inch wedge Parmesan or Romano cheese,
cut into cubes
3 tablespoons chopped fresh basil

Cook the pasta in a saucepan of boiling salted water until al dente. Drain the pasta, reserving 1 cup of the cooking liquid. Heat 2 tablespoons olive oil in a skillet over medium heat. Add the eggplant and sauté for 5 to 8 minutes or just until tender. Remove the eggplant to a bowl and add 1 tablespoon olive oil to the skillet. Add the garlic and sauté until tende; do not brown. Add the tomatoes and cook for 5 to 6 minutes or until softened. Stir in the spaghetti sauce, sugar, salt, pepper and red pepper flakes and simmer for 3 to 5 minutes. Stir in the reserved pasta liquid and eggplant and cook until hot. Remove from the heat and stir in the cheese and basil. Serve over the hot pasta. **Serves 4.**

Bonnie Ross
Grandmother to Ross Clifton '12, Camille Clifton '13
and Bella Clifton '15

To Learn: The starch-enriched water from the
pasta acts as a thickener.

77

Penne à la Vodka

1 onion, chopped
3 garlic cloves, minced
4 teaspoons butter or margarine
1 (16-ounce) can whole tomatoes, drained
1 (8-ounce) can tomato sauce
2/3 cup vodka
1/4 to 1/2 teaspoon crushed red pepper
2/3 cup whipping cream
16 ounces penne, cooked and drained
Freshly grated Parmesan cheese

Sauté the onion and garlic in the butter in a large skillet for 5 minutes or until golden brown. Add the tomatoes and tomato sauce and mix well. Stir in the vodka and crushed red pepper. Stir in the cream and bring to a boil. Add the pasta and mix well. Cook until heated through. Sprinkle with cheese. Serve immediately. **Serves 4 to 6.**

Darlene Miller
Grandmother of Madison Mueller '12 and
Caroline Mueller '15

To Learn: The first recipe for tomatoes and
pasta was made by Ippolito Buonvicino, Duke of Buonvicino.
It was called vermicelli co le pommoddoro.

Italian Pasta Salad

1 tomato, chopped
1 green bell pepper, chopped
1 red bell pepper, chopped
1 bunch green onions, chopped
1 large garlic clove, chopped
10 to 12 kalamata olives
12 to 16 ounces tri-color pasta,
cooked and drained
8 ounces mozzarella cheese, diced
3/4 cup olive oil
1 tablespoon red wine vinegar
Juice of 1/2 lemon
1 tablespoon dried basil, or
3 tablespoons chopped fresh basil
2 teaspoons dried oregano, or
2 tablespoons chopped fresh oregano
Salt and pepper to taste

Combine the tomato, green bell pepper, red bell pepper, green onions, garlic, olives, pasta and cheese in a large bowl and toss to combine. Whisk the olive oil, vinegar, lemon juice, basil, oregano, salt and pepper in a bowl. Add to the pasta mixture and toss to coat. **Serves 8.**

Donna Kiplinger

To Serve: This is a traditional pasta salad. For a variation, add hearts of palm or artichoke hearts.

Greek Pasta Salad

12 ounces rotini, cooked, drained and cooled
1 small green bell pepper,
cut into thin strips
1 small yellow bell pepper,
cut into thin strips
1 small red bell pepper,
cut into thin strips
12 ounces grape tomatoes, cut into halves
1/4 cup pine nuts, toasted
2/3 cup olive oil
3 tablespoons red wine vinegar
2 tablespoons chopped fresh basil
2 tablespoons chopped
green onions
2 tablespoons grated Parmesan cheese
1 1/4 teaspoons salt
1/4 teaspoon pepper
8 ounces tomato basil feta cheese
1/4 teaspoon dried oregano

Combine the pasta, green bell pepper, yellow bell pepper, red bell pepper, tomatoes and pine nuts in a bowl and toss to combine. Whisk the olive oil, vinegar, basil, green onions, Parmesan cheese, salt and pepper in a bowl. Add to the pasta mixture and toss to coat. Add the feta cheese and toss to combine. Sprinkle with oregano. Garnish with fresh basil and serve. **Serves 8.**

Cindy Riesen
Mother of Will Riesen '08 and Matt Riesen '10

Orzo Salad with Roasted Vegetables

1/3 cup good-quality olive oil
1/3 cup fresh lemon juice (about 2 lemons)
1/2 teaspoon kosher salt
Freshly ground pepper to taste
1 red bell pepper, cut into 1-inch pieces
1 yellow bell pepper, cut into 1-inch pieces
1 red onion, cut into 1-inch pieces
2 garlic cloves, minced
1/3 cup good-quality olive oil
1 1/2 teaspoons kosher salt
1/2 teaspoon freshly ground pepper
8 ounces orzo, cooked, drained and kept warm
4 green onions, chopped
1/2 cup pine nuts, toasted
8 ounces good-quality feta cheese,
cut into 1/2-inch cubes
15 basil leaves, cut into thin strips

Whisk 1/3 cup olive oil, the lemon juice and 1/2 teaspoon salt in a bowl and season with pepper. Combine the red bell pepper, yellow bell pepper, onion, garlic, 1/3 cup olive oil, 1 1/2 teaspoons salt and 1/2 teaspoon pepper in a bowl and toss to coat. Spread in a nonstick 10×15-inch baking pan. Roast at 425 degrees for 40 minutes. Remove to a large serving bowl, scraping all of the pan juices into the bowl. Add the hot pasta and the desired amount of lemon juice dressing and toss to coat. Let cool to room temperature. Add the green onions, pine nuts, cheese and basil and toss to combine. Adjust the seasonings to taste. Serve at room temperature. **Serves 8.**

Jill Rojas
Aunt of Blake Crowley '14 and Paige Crowley '16

To Learn: This salad can be made a day ahead. Wait to add the green onions, pine nuts, feta, and basil until just before serving.

Spinach, Feta and Garbanzo Bean Pasta Salad

6 ounces penne or spiral pasta
1/4 cup olive oil
2 tablespoons fresh lemon juice
2 to 4 garlic cloves, minced
1/2 teaspoon salt

1/2 teaspoon pepper
1 cup feta cheese
1 can garbanzo beans, drained
6 cups fresh spinach,
  coarsely chopped

Prepare the pasta according to the package directions; drain and keep warm. Whisk the olive oil, lemon juice, garlic, salt and pepper in a large serving bowl. Add the pasta, cheese, garbanzo beans and spinach and toss to coat. **Serves 8.**

Kelly Suchy
In loving memory of her cousin, Sara Brinson '07

To Serve: You may make in advance and add the spinach just before serving.

Never-Fail Noodles

3 eggs
1/3 cup milk
3/4 tablespoon butter, melted
4 drops of yellow food color

3 cups all-purpose flour
3/4 teaspoon baking powder
1 1/2 teaspoons salt

Beat the eggs in a bowl. Add the milk, butter and food color and mix well. Sift the flour, baking powder and salt into the egg mixture and mix well; the dough will be stiff and somewhat dry. Knead the dough on a floured work surface to form a ball. Roll out the dough with a floured rolling pin to 1/8 inch thick. Let dry for 8 to 10 hours. Cut the dough into 1/4-inch strips. Cook the noodles in a large saucepan of boiling water or chicken broth until tender; drain. **Serves 4 to 6.**

LeAnn Gage
Mother of Garrett Gage '16

Entrées

Entrées

Beef Tenderloin with
   Blue Cheese, Cremini
   Mushrooms and Red Wine
Standing Rib Roast with
   Roasted Potatoes and
   Horseradish Sauce
Flaming Brandy Tenderloin Steaks
Incredible Whiskey Steaks
Dr. Pepper-Marinated Tri-Tip Steak
Welker Brothers' Tailgate
   Barbecue
Green Hills Brisket
Famous Tenderloin Chili
Brown Sugar Molasses Ham
Saturday Night Pork Tenderloin
Peppered Pork Tenderloin
Honey Pork Loin with
   Sweet Potatoes
Dry Rub Baby Back Ribs
Sweet-and-Sour Pork Ribs
Chicken with Peach and
   Avocado Salsa
Noah's Grilled Jalapeño Lime
   Chicken

Chicken Enchiladas
Artichoke and Feta Chicken
Goat Cheese-Stuffed Chicken
Chicken with Mushroom White
   Wine Sauce
Chicken Potpie
Slow-Cooker Barbecued Chicken
Asian Garlic Chicken
Mallu Murg
Champagne Shrimp Risotto
Pan-Seared Tuna with
   Ginger-Shiitake Cream Sauce
Fresh Salmon Cakes
Pepper-Crusted Maple-Glazed
   Salmon
Pan-Fried Tilapia
Scott Griffin's Steak Seasoning
Boat Dock Steak Marinade
Blender Béarnaise Sauce
Easy Hollandaise Sauce
Sweet Hot Mustard
Blue Cheese Mustard Sauce
Garlic Herb Aïoli
Jolly Red Relish

Beef Tenderloin with Blue Cheese, Cremini Mushrooms and Red Wine

Sauce

1 large yellow onion, chopped
2 tablespoons olive oil
1 tablespoon unsalted butter
2 tablespoons tomato paste
2 garlic cloves, minced
2 cups dry red wine
1 (14-ounce) can no-salt-added beef broth
5 sprigs of fresh thyme
8 ounces cremini mushrooms
2 tablespoons unsalted butter
1 tablespoon olive oil

Beef

1/4 cup olive oil
1 tablespoon sea salt
1 tablespoon freshly ground pepper
1 (3- to 4-pound) beef tenderloin, trimmed
6 ounces Maytag blue cheese or Gorgonzola cheese, crumbled

For the sauce, sauté the onion in 2 tablespoons olive oil and 1 tablespoon butter in a skillet until golden brown. Stir in the tomato paste. Cook to a rich brown color, stirring constantly. Add the garlic and sauté for 1 minute. Add the wine and cook, scraping up any brown bits from the bottom of the pan. Stir in the broth and thyme. Simmer for 20 minutes or until the liquid is reduced by half. Strain the sauce into a bowl. Sauté the mushrooms in 2 tablespoons butter and 1 tablespoon olive oil in a skillet until tender. Add to the sauce and keep warm.

For the beef, mix the olive oil, salt and pepper in a bowl. Rub over all sides of the tenderloin. Cook in a hot ovenproof skillet for 2 to 3 minutes per side or until brown. Roast at 450 degrees for 30 to 40 minutes or until a meat thermometer inserted into the thickest part of the tenderloin registers 130 degrees for medium-rare. Remove to a cutting board; cover with foil. Let stand for 10 to 15 minutes. Slice and serve with the wine sauce and cheese. **Serves 10 to 12.**

Christina Mayo
Mother of Delaney Mayo '16, Dylan Mayo '20 and Daylee Mayo '23

To Lead: Pairing this with the Champagne Salad with Pear and Goat Cheese Tartlets (page 32) creates a delightful blend of flavors.

Standing Rib Roast with Roasted Potatoes and Horseradish Sauce

3/4 cup sour cream
1 to 2 tablespoons prepared horseradish
1/4 teaspoon dry mustard
1 (4- to 6-pound) standing rib roast
Salt and pepper to taste
All-purpose flour
8 to 10 red potatoes, parboiled and cut into halves

Mix the sour cream, horseradish and mustard in a bowl. Chill, covered, until serving time. Place the roast, fat side up, in a shallow roasting pan. Season liberally with salt and pepper and coat with flour on all sides. Roast at 450 degrees for 20 minutes. Reduce the oven temperature to 325 degrees. Roast for 20 minutes per pound or until a meat thermometer inserted into the thickest part of the roast registers 130 degrees for medium-rare. Add the potatoes, cut side down, for the last hour of roasting. Serve with the horseradish sauce. Ask the butcher to remove the bones and tie them back on for easier carving. **Serves 8 to 10.**

Linda Bell
Great-aunt of Britni Griffin '12 and Chandler Griffin '16

To Lead: This makes a beautiful presentation!
Serve with Spinach-Stuffed Tomatoes (page 46).

Flaming Brandy Tenderloin Steaks

1 garlic clove
4 (2-inch-thick) tenderloin steaks, trimmed
Salt and coarsely ground pepper to taste
1/4 cup (1/2 stick) butter
1/2 cup brandy or cognac
Additional brandy or cognac
2/3 cup heavy cream

Cut the thick end off the garlic and rub the clove over all sides of the steaks. Sprinkle each steak liberally with salt and pepper, pressing the pepper into the meat. Place on a plate and chill for 3 hours or longer. Heat the butter in a heavy skillet until it stops foaming. Add the steaks and cook on both sides to rare. Pour 1/2 cup brandy over the steaks. Ignite the brandy with a long match and let the flames subside. Remove the steaks to baking pan in a warm oven. Add a small amount of brandy to the skillet. Ignite the brandy with a long match and let the flames subside. Stir in the cream. Cook until reduced to the desired consistency, stirring constantly. Serve over the steaks. **Serves 4.**

Pat Griffin
Grandmother of Britni Griffin '12 and Chandler Griffin '16

To Serve: This makes a delectable tableside presentation. Your guests will be impressed.

Incredible Whiskey Steaks

2 tablespoons olive oil
2 tablespoons butter
6 (1/2-inch-thick) tenderloin steaks
Salt and pepper to taste
2 tablespoons minced shallots
1 tablespoon butter
1/2 cup beef broth
1/3 cup bourbon
3 tablespoons butter, softened

Heat the oil and 2 tablespoons butter in a skillet over medium-high heat. Add the steaks and cook for 3 to 4 minutes per side or to the desired doneness. Remove the steaks to a warm platter and season with salt and pepper; keep warm. Drain the skillet. Sauté the shallots in 1 tablespoon butter in the skillet until tender. Add the broth and boil for 2 minutes, scraping up any brown bits from the bottom of the pan. Stir in the bourbon and boil for 2 minutes longer. Remove from the heat and stir in 3 tablespoons butter. Pour over the steaks and serve. **Serves 6.**

Sally Saunders
Grandmother of Trent Saunders '13, Sayde Saunders '17,
Anna Denner '12 and Salli Denner '16

To Serve: This sauce would be delicious on any cut of meat.
Just adjust your cooking time according to the cut.

Dr. Pepper-Marinated Tri-Tip Steak

3 pounds tri-tip steak or flank steak
1 to 2 cans Dr. Pepper soda
1/2 cup kosher salt
1/2 cup coarsely ground pepper
1/2 cup packed brown sugar
2 tablespoons garlic powder

Place the steak in a sealable plastic bag. Pour the soda over the steak. Seal tightly and turn to coat. Marinate in the refrigerator for 2 to 10 hours. Remove the steak and discard the marinade. Mix the salt, pepper, brown sugar and garlic powder in a bowl. Season the steak liberally with the brown sugar rub mixture, pressing it into the meat. Store the remaining rub in an airtight container for another use. Grill the steak over medium-high heat for 7 minutes per side or until a meat thermometer inserted in the thickest part of the steak registers 140 degrees for medium-rare. Remove the meat to a cutting board and let stand for 10 minutes. Slice across the grain and serve. **Serves 8 to 10.**

Bob Jarman
Father of Meg Jarman '12 and Jennings Jarman '15

To Serve: The contributor prefers tri-tip steak over flank steak due to flavor. Serve as fajitas, on sandwiches, or just by itself.

Welker Brothers' Tailgate Barbecue

1/2 cup barbecue seasoning
1 (28-ounce) can tomato sauce
1/4 cup packed brown sugar
1/4 cup lemon juice
1/2 cup tomato juice
1 tablespoon liquid smoke
2 tablespoons Worcestershire sauce
2 1/2 pounds boneless beef chuck roast
2 1/2 pounds boneless pork roast

Mix the barbecue seasoning, tomato sauce, brown sugar, lemon juice, tomato juice, liquid smoke and Worcestershire sauce in a bowl. Pour over the beef and pork in a large baking dish. Bake, covered, at 300 degrees for 5 to 6 hours. **Serves 10 to 12.**

Shelley Welker
Mother of Lee Welker '95 and Wes Welker '00

To Serve: Pile on a large platter and serve with miniature buns and extra sauce—a perfect way to celebrate the big game.

Green Hills Brisket

1 (4- to 5-pound) beef brisket
2 teaspoons Worcestershire sauce
$1/4$ cup liquid smoke
1 teaspoon onion salt
1 teaspoon garlic salt
2 teaspoons celery seeds
Salt and pepper to taste
2 cups packed brown sugar
1 cup ketchup
$1^1/2$ cups vinegar
24 dashes of soy sauce
16 dashes of Worcestershire sauce

Place the brisket in a sealable plastic bag. Mix 2 teaspoons Worcestershire sauce, the liquid smoke, onion salt, garlic salt and celery seeds in a bowl and pour over the meat. Seal tightly and turn to coat. Marinate in the refrigerator for 8 to 10 hours. Remove the brisket to a large sheet of foil and discard the marinade. Season the brisket with salt and pepper. Seal in the foil and place in a baking dish. Bake at 350 degrees for 1 hour. Reduce the oven temperature to 300 degrees and bake for 2 hours longer. Open the foil carefully and drain the grease. Mix the brown sugar, ketchup, vinegar, soy sauce and 16 of dashes Worcestershire sauce in a bowl. Pour one-fourth of the brown sugar sauce over the brisket and reseal the foil. Bake at 300 degrees until the meat is tender. Serve with the remaining sauce. **Serves 10 to 12.**

Josie Stephenson
Mother of Elise Stephenson '16, Emory Stephenson '19 and
Ford Stephenson '21

Famous Tenderloin Chili

2 pounds Italian sausage, casings removed
1 onion, chopped
4 garlic cloves, minced
Olive oil
2 pounds beef tenderloin, ground
2 green bell peppers, chopped
2 red bell peppers, chopped
6 jalapeño chiles, seeded and chopped
2 (28-ounce) cans petite-cut diced tomatoes
1 (15-ounce) can tomato sauce

1 (28-ounce) can crushed tomatoes
1 can kidney beans
1 cup dry red wine, or 1 (12-ounce) can beer
1 cup chopped fresh parsley
2 tablespoons tomato paste
6 tablespoons chili powder
2 tablespoons cumin
2 tablespoons oregano
1 tablespoon basil
1 tablespoon baking cocoa
1 1/2 teaspoons fennel seeds
Salt and pepper to taste

Brown the sausage in a skillet, stirring until crumbly; drain. Sauté the onion and garlic in a small amount of olive oil in a large saucepan until tender. Add the ground tenderloin and cook, stirring until crumbly; drain. Stir in the sausage, green bell peppers, red bell peppers and jalapeño chiles. Cook for 15 minutes, stirring occasionally. Add the diced tomatoes, tomato sauce, crushed tomatoes, kidney beans, wine, parsley, tomato paste, chili powder, cumin, oregano, basil, baking cocoa, fennel seeds, salt and pepper and mix well. Simmer for 2 hours or until of the desired consistency, stirring occasionally. **Serves 18 to 20.**

State Senator Cliff Branan '80

To Serve: You may add cayenne pepper or paprika for a different flavor.

Brown Sugar Molasses Ham

1 (12- to 14-pound) ham	2 tablespoons prepared
1 cup water	mustard
2 cups packed brown sugar	1 teaspoon allspice
1/2 cup blackstrap molasses	

Wrap the ham completely in foil and place in a covered roasting pan. Add the water to the bottom of the pan. Bake at 300 degrees for 20 minutes for the first pound and 15 minutes per pound for the remaining time. Remove the foil from the ham and return the ham to the roasting pan. Combine the brown sugar, molasses, mustard and allspice in a bowl and mix well. Spread over the ham. Bake at 450 degrees for 15 to 20 minutes. **Serves 20 to 30.**

Mary Jo Schneider
Grandmother of Davis Angel '14

Saturday Night Pork Tenderloin

1 (2-pound) pork tenderloin	6 tablespoons chopped
1/2 cup packed brown sugar	green onions
6 tablespoons bourbon	3 tablespoons vegetable oil or
1/4 cup soy sauce	canola oil

Place the pork in a sealable plastic bag. Mix the brown sugar, bourbon, soy sauce, green onions and oil in a bowl and pour over the pork. Seal tightly and turn to coat. Marinate in the refrigerator for 8 to 10 hours. Remove the pork and marinade to a roasting pan or 9×13-inch baking dish and let stand to come to room temperature. Bake at 325 degrees for 45 minutes or until a meat thermometer inserted into the thickest part of the tenderloin registers 155 degrees, basting every 15 minutes. Slice the pork and serve with the marinade. This marinade works well with chicken, or use with salmon, marinating for 1 1/2 hours. **Serves 4 to 5.**

Julie Jones Corley
Mother of Sam Corley '15, John Corley '19 and Caroline Corley '19

Peppered Pork Tenderloin

Sauce	Pork
1/2 cup mayonnaise	2 (1-pound) pork tenderloins
1/4 cup sour cream	2 cups canola oil
1/4 teaspoon salt	1/3 cup soy sauce
1 tablespoon pepper	1/4 cup honey
1 tablespoon garlic powder	1 tablespoon onion powder
2 teaspoons Dijon mustard	1 tablespoon garlic powder
1 teaspoon Worcestershire sauce	Seasoned salt to taste
	Cracked pepper to taste

For the sauce, combine the mayonnaise, sour cream, salt, pepper, garlic powder, Dijon mustard and Worcestershire sauce in a bowl and mix well. Chill until serving time.

For the pork, place the tenderloins in a sealable plastic bag. Mix the canola oil, soy sauce, honey, onion powder and garlic powder in a bowl; reserve 1/2 cup. Pour the remaining oil mixture over the pork. Seal tightly and turn to coat. Marinate in the refrigerator for 2 to 24 hours. Remove the pork and discard the marinade. Mix the seasoned salt and pepper together. Coat the pork in the pepper mixture. Grill over hot coals for 20 to 40 minutes or until cooked though, turning and basting frequently with the 1/2 cup reserved marinade. Slice the pork and serve with the sauce. This marinade makes enough to marinate up to six pork tenderloins. **Serves 8.**

Kara Brown
Mother of Callan Brown '06 and Travis Brown '08

To Lead: We loved that you could do
*the preparation ahead. Serve with the Baby Spinach Salad
with Pears and Gorgonzola (page 31).*

Honey Pork Loin with Sweet Potatoes

Spiced Butter

1 cup (2 sticks) butter,
softened
2 tablespoons honey
1/2 teaspoon cinnamon
1/2 teaspoon ginger
1/4 teaspoon nutmeg
1/4 teaspoon cayenne pepper

Pork

1 (4-pound) boneless
pork loin, trimmed
1/3 cup olive oil
3 garlic cloves, cut into halves
2 tablespoons dried sage
2 teaspoons salt
1 teaspoon pepper
1/3 cup honey
1/3 cup red wine vinegar
4 sweet potatoes, scrubbed
and skins pierced

For the spiced butter, beat the butter, honey, cinnamon, ginger, nutmeg and cayenne pepper in a bowl. Chill or freeze, covered, until serving time.

For the pork, rub the pork with some of the olive oil. Rub the cut side of the garlic over the pork. Rub the sage, salt and pepper over the pork. Place the pork in a sealable plastic bag and add the remaining olive oil and the garlic halves. Seal tightly and turn to coat. Marinate in the refrigerator for 8 to 10 hours. Remove the pork to a roasting pan and discard the marinade. Mix the honey and vinegar in a bowl. Pour half the vinegar mixture over the pork, reserving the remaining half. Place the pork in a 375-degree oven and arrange the sweet potatoes directly on the oven rack. Bake for 20 minutes. Pour the remaining vinegar mixture over the pork. Bake for 20 to 30 minutes longer or until a meat thermometer inserted into the thickest part of the pork registers 160 degrees and the potatoes are very tender. Baste the pork with the pan juices and let stand for 8 minutes. Peel the potatoes and remove to a bowl. Mash with 2 tablespoons of the spiced butter. Mound the potatoes onto the center of serving plates. Cut the pork into 1/4-inch-thick slices and arrange around the potatoes. Melt the remaining spiced butter in a saucepan and drizzle over the pork. **Serves 8 to 10.**

Reba Gallaspy
Grandmother of Banning Fudge '09

Dry Rub Baby Back Ribs

2 slabs baby back pork ribs
1 cup packed brown sugar
1 tablespoon paprika
1/2 teaspoon cumin
1/2 teaspoon black pepper
1 teaspoon (or more) cayenne pepper
1 tablespoon chili powder
1/2 teaspoon salt
1/2 teaspoon dried oregano

Pat excess moisture from the ribs with paper towels. Mix the brown sugar, paprika, cumin, black pepper, cayenne pepper, chili powder, salt and oregano in a bowl. Cover the ribs completely with the spice mixture to 1/8 inch thick, Wrap the ribs in plastic wrap and chill for 1 hour or longer. Remove the ribs from the refrigerator and let stand for 30 minutes before grilling. Place the ribs on a sheet of foil on a grill over low heat. Grill 1 to 11/2 hours or until the meat separates easily from the bone. **Serves 6 to 8.**

Lance Cook '98

To Learn: Keep a squirt bottle filled with
*water near the grill. At the first signs of a flare-up, move the ribs
over and give the flames a squirt!*

Sweet-and-Sour Pork Ribs

1 cup ketchup
1/2 cup white vinegar
1/2 onion, chopped
1/4 cup dark unsulfured molasses
1/4 cup honey
1/4 cup currant jelly
2 tablespoons soy sauce
1 tablespoon chopped garlic
1 teaspoon dry mustard
1 teaspoon ginger
3 to 31/2 pounds spareribs,
cut into 2-rib sections, trimmed

Mix the ketchup, vinegar, onion, molasses, honey, jelly, soy sauce, garlic, mustard and ginger in a heavy large saucepan. Bring to a boil over medium-high heat, stirring occasionally. Reduce the heat to medium and simmer for 5 minutes. Add the spareribs and stir to coat. Simmer, covered, for 45 minutes or until the spareribs are almost tender. Remove the spareribs with tongs to a shallow baking pan. Bake at 350 degrees for 10 minutes. Boil the sauce in the saucepan for 10 minutes or until reduced to 2 cups. Spoon enough of the sauce over the ribs to thickly coat each rib. Bake for 20 minutes longer or until the ribs are glazed and very tender. Serve immediately with the remaining sauce on the side. **Serves 4.**

Shirley Remondino
Grandmother of Molly Remondino '14 and Annie Remondino '18

Chicken with Peach and Avocado Salsa

Salsa

1 peach, peeled, pitted and diced
1 small avocado, diced
1 tomato, peeled, seeded and diced
3 tablespoons chopped red onion
2 tablespoons chopped cilantro
3 tablespoons fresh lime juice
2 teaspoons olive oil
1/4 teaspoon crushed red pepper flakes

Chicken

6 boneless skinless chicken breasts
4 teaspoons garlic pepper seasoning
Juice of 1 orange
Juice of 1 lime
2 tablespoons olive oil
1 teaspoon dried oregano

For the salsa, mix the peach, avocado, tomato, onion and cilantro in a bowl. Whisk the lime juice, olive oil and red pepper flakes in a bowl. Pour over the peach mixture and stir gently.

For the chicken, arrange the chicken in a shallow glass dish. Rub all sides of the chicken with the garlic pepper seasoning. Pour the orange juice and lime juice evenly over the chicken and drizzle with the olive oil. Crush the oregano with your fingers and sprinkle over the top. Chill, covered, for 30 minutes, turning once. Remove the chicken and discard the marinade. Cook the chicken in a nonstick skillet over medium heat until golden brown and cooked through, turning once. You may also grill the chicken. Serve topped with the salsa. **Serves 6.**

Kelly Brewer
Godmother of Paige Crowley '16

Noah's Grilled Jalapeño Lime Chicken

4 boneless skinless chicken breasts
2 teaspoons grated lime zest
1/4 cup lime juice
1/4 cup olive oil
2 tablespoons chopped fresh cilantro
1/2 teaspoon sugar
1/2 teaspoon salt
1 small jalapeño chile, seeded and finely chopped
(or include seeds for more heat)
1 garlic clove, minced

Pound the chicken between sheets of waxed paper to 1/4 inch thick. Place the chicken in a sealable plastic bag. Mix the lime zest, lime juice, olive oil, cilantro, sugar, salt, jalapeño chile and garlic in a bowl and pour over the chicken. Seal tightly and turn to coat. Marinate in the refrigerator for 30 minutes to 24 hours. Remove the chicken and discard the marinade. Grill over medium heat for 8 to 10 minutes or until a meat thermometer inserted into the thickest part of the chicken registers 170 degrees, turning once. **Serves 4.**

Kristin McAdams
Mother of Noah McAdams '20

Chicken Enchiladas

3 cups cubed cooked chicken breasts
2 cups (8 ounces) shredded Pepper Jack cheese
1/2 cup sour cream
1 (4 ounce) can chopped green chiles, drained
8 to 10 (8-inch) flour tortillas
Nonstick cooking spray
1 cup sour cream
1 cup green taco sauce

Combine the chicken, cheese, 1/2 cup sour cream and the green chiles in a bowl and mix well. Spoon the chicken mixture evenly over each tortilla and roll up. Arrange the enchiladas in a lightly greased 9×13-inch baking dish. Coat the enchiladas with nonstick cooking spray. Bake at 350 degrees for 35 to 40 minutes or until golden brown. Mix 1 cup sour cream and the taco sauce in a bowl and spoon over the enchiladas. Garnish with chopped green onions and serve. **Serves 8 to 10.**

Julie Gist
Aunt of Blake Crowley '14 and Paige Crowley '16

To Serve: Accompany this dish with
*Simply Salsa (page 26) or Cherry Pepper Salsa (page 27) and a
huge bowl of warm tortilla chips. What's not to like?*

Artichoke and Feta Chicken

1 teaspoon olive oil
3/4 cup artichoke hearts, chopped
1/4 cup minced shallots
1/4 cup feta cheese
1/2 teaspoon herbes de Provence
1/8 teaspoon salt
1/8 teaspoon pepper
4 (4-ounce) boneless skinless chicken breasts
1 teaspoon olive oil
1/8 teaspoon salt
1/8 teaspoon pepper
1/2 teaspoon herbes de Provence
1 cup fat-free, reduced-sodium chicken broth
2 tablespoons lemon juice
2 teaspoons cornstarch

Heat 1 teaspoon olive oil in a nonstick skillet over medium heat. Add the artichoke hearts and shallots and sauté for 4 minutes. Remove to a bowl and let cool. Stir in the cheese, 1/2 teaspoon herbes de Provence, 1/8 teaspoon salt and 1/8 teaspoon pepper. Cut a horizontal slit into the thickest portion of each chicken breast to create a pocket. Stuff 2 tablespoons of the artichoke mixture into each pocket. Heat 1 teaspoon olive oil in a large nonstick skillet over medium heat. Add the chicken and sprinkle with 1/8 teaspoon salt and 1/8 teaspoon pepper. Cook for 6 minutes per side or until the chicken is cooked through. Remove the chicken to a platter and keep warm. Add 1/2 teaspoon herbes de Provence and the broth to the skillet and bring to a boil. Mix the lemon juice and cornstarch in a bowl. Whisk into the broth mixture in the skillet. Cook for 1 minute or until thickened. Add the chicken to the skillet and cook, covered, for 2 minutes or until the chicken is heated through. **Serves 4.**

Sarah Stringer Butler '91 and Doug Butler '88

To Learn: Choose plump chicken breasts to make cutting the pocket easy!

Goat Cheese-Stuffed Chicken

4 boneless chicken breasts
8 slices bacon, crisp-cooked and crumbled
8 ounces plain or herb-flavored goat cheese
4 to 8 large fresh basil leaves
1 cup all-purpose flour
2 eggs
1 cup Italian-style bread crumbs
Vegetable oil

Cut a horizontal slit into the thickest portion of each chicken breast to create a pocket. Fill each pocket with one-fourth of the bacon, one-fourth of the cheese and one to two basil leaves. Beat the eggs lightly in a shallow dish. Coat the chicken breasts in the flour. Coat in the eggs and then coat in the bread crumbs. Heat a small amount of oil in a skillet. Add the chicken. Cook for 8 to 10 minutes per side or until the chicken is cooked through. **Serves 4.**

Trent Cook '01

To Lead: Serve with Jackson Salad (page 34). This dish is truly special served on a platter with a chiffonade of basil.

Chicken with Mushroom White Wine Sauce

3 whole chicken breasts, split and boned
1 (8-ounce) can sliced mushrooms
2 chicken bouillon cubes
2 to 3 tablespoons lemon juice
$1/4$ cup dry white wine
$1/2$ cup chopped celery
Salt and pepper to taste

$1/2$ cup milk
2 tablespoons soy sauce
$1/2$ teaspoon poultry seasoning
5 tablespoons all-purpose flour
7 tablespoons water
1 (8-ounce) can mushroom pieces, drained
$1/4$ cup (1 ounce) grated Parmesan cheese

Arrange the chicken in a greased Dutch oven. Drain the sliced mushrooms, reserving the liquid. Set the mushrooms aside and pour the reserved mushroom liquid into a 1-cup measuring cup. Add enough water to make $1/2$ cup and pour into a saucepan. Bring to a boil and add the bouillon cubes. Cook until the bouillon cubes are dissolved, stirring constantly. Stir in the lemon juice, wine and celery. Pour over the chicken and sprinkle with salt and pepper. Bake, covered, at 400 degrees for 15 to 20 minutes or until the chicken is cooked through; do not overcook. Remove the chicken to a platter using tongs and keep warm. Heat the liquid in the Dutch oven over low heat. Stir in the milk, soy sauce, and poultry seasoning. Mix the flour and water in a bowl. Stir into the milk mixture. Cook until thickened, stirring constantly. Stir in the sliced mushrooms and mushroom pieces and season with salt and pepper. Add the chicken and cook until heated through. Sprinkle with the cheese. Cover and keep warm until serving time. **Serves 6.**

Margaret Reynolds Hoge '74
Mother of Katie Hoge '06 and Cort Hoge '08

To Serve: You may substitute fresh mushrooms. Slice a small carton of mushrooms. Sauté in 2 tablespoons butter. The test kitchen felt they had a better texture.

Chicken Potpie

1 cup all-purpose flour
1/2 teaspoon salt
1/3 cup plus 1 tablespoon
  shortening
2 to 3 tablespoons cold water
1 cup chopped onion
1 cup chopped celery
1 cup chopped carrot

1/2 cup (1 stick) butter
1/2 cup all-purpose flour
2 cups chicken broth
1 cup half-and-half
1 teaspoon salt
1/4 teaspoon pepper
4 cups chopped cooked
  chicken

Mix 1 cup flour and 1/2 teaspoon salt in a bowl. Cut in the shortening with a pastry blender until crumbly. Sprinkle with the cold water and stir with a fork until the mixture forms a ball. Wrap in plastic wrap and chill. Sauté the onion, celery and carrot in the butter in a skillet for 10 minutes. Stir in 1/2 cup flour. Cook for 1 minute, stirring constantly. Mix the broth and half-and-half in bowl. Stir into the vegetable mixture gradually. Cook over medium heat until thick and bubbly, stirring constantly. Stir in 1 teaspoon salt and the pepper. Stir in the chicken. Spoon into a shallow 2-quart baking dish. Roll out the chilled dough on a floured surface. Fit the dough over the baking dish, pressing the edges to seal. Cut slits over the top of the pastry. Bake at 400 degrees for 40 minutes or until the crust is golden brown. **Serves 6.**

Wilma Mastell
Grandmother of Baillie Miller '15, Blake Miller '20 and Gavin Mastell '13

To Learn: To transport the fresh pastry onto the top of your dish, simply roll the pastry onto your rolling pin. Place over your casserole, and then unroll. It is a great way to keep it from tearing.

Slow-Cooker Barbecued Chicken

4 pounds boneless skinless chicken breasts,
cut into pieces
Vegetable oil
1 onion, chopped
1/4 cup chopped green bell pepper
1 cup ketchup
1 to 2 tablespoons prepared mustard
1 tablespoon Worcestershire sauce
1 tablespoon lemon juice
1 tablespoon vinegar
3 tablespoons brown sugar
1/4 cup water
1/2 teaspoon salt
1/8 teaspoon pepper

Cook the chicken in a small amount of oil in a skillet until light brown. Remove the chicken to a slow cooker. Layer the onion and bell pepper over the chicken. Combine the ketchup, mustard, Worcestershire sauce, lemon juice, vinegar, brown sugar, water, salt and pepper in a bowl and mix well. Pour over the chicken. Cook on Low for 6 hours or cook on High for 4 hours or until the chicken is cooked through. **Serves 10 to 12.**

Ann Jones-Wilson
Great-aunt of Jack Hansing '16 and Lilly Hansing '18

To Serve: Serve the chicken and sauce over rice.

Asian Garlic Chicken

8 chicken thighs or breasts
1 tablespoon peanut oil or olive oil
6 to 8 garlic cloves, coarsely chopped
1/4 teaspoon hot red pepper flakes
1/2 cup rice vinegar
1/4 cup soy sauce
3 tablespoons honey

Trim the fat from the chicken and remove the skin, if desired. Spray a heavy skillet with nonstick cooking spray and add the peanut oil. Heat the oil over medium-high heat. Add the chicken and cook until brown on all sides, adding the garlic and red pepper flakes near the end of browning. Stir in the vinegar, soy sauce and honey. Cook for 10 minutes or until the chicken is cooked through and the sauce is slightly reduced, watching carefully so that the sauce is not completely reduced. Remove chicken breasts first if cooking thighs and breasts. Serve with rice.
Serves 4 to 6.

Bob Remondino
Father of Molly Remondino '14 and Annie Remondino '18

To Learn: This mouth-watering chicken dish
was a first-place winner in the Gilroy Garlic Recipe Cook-off.
It's simple and quick to prepare.

Mallu Murg

Masala
1 to 2 teaspoons star anise
2 to 3 cardamom pods
2 to 3 teaspoons whole cloves
1 (^{1}/2-inch) cinnamon stick
^{1}/2 teaspoon poppy seeds
2 tablespoons ground cashews
(optional)

Chicken
2 medium to large sweet
onions, finely chopped
2 tablespoons canola oil or
olive oil

3 garlic cloves, minced
1 (^{1}/2-inch) piece fresh ginger,
finely chopped
1 to 3 green chiles,
finely chopped
1 tomato, finely chopped
1 cup water
2 pounds boneless skinless
chicken, cut into
1-inch pieces
2 large potatoes, cubed
Salt to taste

For the masala, grind the star anise, cardamom, cloves, cinnamon stick, poppy seeds and cashews into a bowl and mix well.

For the chicken, sauté the onions in the canola oil in a skillet until golden brown. Add the garlic, ginger, green chiles and tomato and sauté for 5 minutes. Add the masala and sauté for 5 minutes over medium-low heat. Stir in the water. Season the chicken and potatoes with salt and add to the skillet. Cook over medium heat for 45 minutes or until the chicken is cooked though, adding more water if needed. Garnish with chopped cilantro and serve with rice or bread. For added flavor and moistness, marinate the chicken in a mixture of ginger-garlic paste (available at Indian grocery stores) and yogurt. Chill, covered, for 4 to 6 hours before cooking. **Serves 4 to 6.**

Pushpa Joseph
Mother of Nathan Joseph '14 and Naveen Joseph '18

To Learn: This is a traditional Indian dish.

Champagne Shrimp Risotto

1/2 cup sliced green onions
1/4 cup (1/2 stick) butter
2 1/2 cups arborio rice
2 cups dry Champagne
2 (14-ounce) cans chicken broth
1/2 cup (2 ounces) grated Parmesan cheese
Pinch of garlic powder
Salt and pepper to taste

3 tablespoons butter
2 garlic cloves, minced
1 tablespoon fresh rosemary
1/4 teaspoon cayenne pepper
2 1/2 tablespoons Worcestershire sauce
3/4 cup dry Champagne
1 tablespoon lemon juice
1 pound unpeeled fresh shrimp

Sauté the green onions in 1/4 cup butter in a saucepan over medium heat for 1 minute. Add the rice and sauté for 2 minutes. Stir in 2 cups Champagne and simmer until the liquid has evaporated. Cook for a few minutes, stirring constantly. Add the broth. Cook for 15 minutes or until the rice is tender and the mixture is creamy, stirring constantly. Stir in the cheese, garlic powder, salt and pepper. Simmer for 5 minutes, adding additional broth if the mixture is too thick. Keep warm.

Melt 3 tablespoons butter in a heavy skillet over high heat. Add the garlic, rosemary and cayenne pepper and sauté for 30 seconds. Stir in Worcestershire sauce, 3/4 cup Champagne and the lemon juice. Boil for 5 minutes or until the liquid is reduced by one-half. Stir in the shrimp and simmer for 3 minutes or until the shrimp turn pink. Stir in the risotto and serve. **Serves 6 to 8.**

Claire Riggs
Mother of Madalyn Riggs '17

To Serve: Serve with a crispy loaf of French bread.

Pan-Seared Tuna with Ginger-Shiitake Cream Sauce

6 (6-ounce) tuna steaks
Pepper to taste
2 tablespoons peanut oil
3 tablespoons butter
2 to 3 green onions, sliced
1/4 cup chopped cilantro
2 tablespoons chopped fresh ginger
4 garlic cloves, chopped
8 ounces fresh shiitake mushrooms,
stems removed and caps sliced
6 tablespoons soy sauce
1 1/2 cups whipping cream
3 tablespoons fresh lime juice

Season one side of the tuna steaks with pepper. Heat the peanut oil in a heavy skillet over high heat. Add the tuna, peppered side down, and cook for 2 minutes. Turn the tuna over and cook for 2 minutes longer for rare. Remove the tuna steaks to a shallow baking pan using tongs. Keep warm in a 200-degree oven. Add the butter, green onions, cilantro, ginger and garlic to the skillet and sauté for 30 seconds or until fragrant. Stir in the sliced mushroom caps and soy sauce and simmer for 30 seconds. Stir in the cream. Simmer for 3 minutes or until the mixture coats the back of a spoon. Stir in the lime juice. Spoon the sauce onto serving plates and top with the tuna. Garnish with lime wedges and cilantro sprigs. **Serves 6.**

Megan Cramer Christensen '90

To Learn: To remove the thin outer skin from ginger, slightly scrape the surface with the tip of a spoon.

Fresh Salmon Cakes

1/2 cup mayonnaise
2 tablespoons chopped cilantro
1/2 teaspoon grated lime zest
1 tablespoon fresh lime juice
Dash of salt
1 pound skinless salmon fillets, cut into 1/2-inch pieces
1/4 cup crumbled butter crackers
1/4 cup heavy cream
1/4 cup finely chopped red onion
1 tablespoon minced fresh dill weed, or 1 1/2 teaspoons dried dill weed
1 tablespoon Dijon mustard
1 egg, beaten
1 garlic clove, minced
1/2 teaspoon Tabasco sauce, or to taste
1/4 teaspoon salt
1/2 cup all-purpose flour
2 tablespoons extra-virgin olive oil

Combine the mayonnaise, cilantro, lime zest, lime juice and dash of salt in a bowl and mix well. Chill, covered, for 30 minutes. Combine the salmon, cracker crumbs, cream, onion, dill weed, Dijon mustard, egg, garlic, Tabasco sauce and 1/4 teaspoon salt in a bowl and mix gently to combine. Form gently into four 1/2-cup patties. Coat each patty lightly in the flour. Heat the olive oil in a 12-inch nonstick skillet over medium heat until hot but not smoking. Add the patties and cook for 10 minutes or until golden brown, turning once. Remove the patties to a baking sheet. Bake at 350 degrees for 10 minutes. Serve with the cilantro lime mayonnaise. **Serves 4.**

Gladys Collison
Grandmother of Sydney Collison '14, Macy Collison '16 and
Tori Collison '19

To Serve: This can be served with fresh vegetables and potatoes or on a bun with tomatoes and lettuce.

Pepper-Crusted Maple-Glazed Salmon

3/4 cup maple syrup
1/4 cup soy sauce
4 (6-ounce) skinless salmon fillets
1/2 teaspoon peanut oil or spritz of oil spray
1/4 cup coarsely ground pepper

Combine the maple syrup and soy sauce in a bowl and mix well. Pour over the salmon in a small deep bowl or in a sealable plastic bag and seal the bag. Marinate the salmon in the refrigerator for 4 to 24 hours, turning the salmon every few hours. Remove the salmon from the marinade and discard the marinade. Spread the peanut oil over a 10×10-inch piece of foil. Spread the pepper over a small plate. Press the top side of the salmon into the pepper to coat. Arrange the salmon, peppered side up, on the foil. Bake at 500 degrees, with the foil directly on the top rack, for 7 minutes or until the fish begins to flake. **Serves 4.**

Diane Surtees
Mother of Bailey Surtees '13 and Monica Surtees '15

To Serve: This can also be served as an appetizer
with toast points, capers, and tomatoes.

Pan-Fried Tilapia

2 eggs, beaten
1/4 cup milk
1 cup all-purpose flour
3 tablespoons grated lemon zest, or to taste
1/2 teaspoon salt
1/4 teaspoon paprika
Dash of pepper
4 tilapia fillets
2 tablespoons vegetable oil
1/4 cup (1/2 stick) butter
1/2 cup sliced green onions
3 tablespoons lemon juice

Mix the eggs and milk in a shallow bowl. Mix the flour, lemon zest, salt, paprika and pepper in a shallow dish. Dip the tilapia into the egg mixture and then coat in the seasoned flour. Arrange the coated fillets on a waxed paper-lined plate and chill for 20 minutes. Heat the oil in a skillet. Add the fillets and cook for 4 minutes per side or until golden brown. Remove the fillets to a platter and keep warm. Wipe out the skillet and return to the heat. Add the butter, green onions and lemon juice and bring to a simmer. Cook for a few minutes, stirring occasionally. Serve over the tilapia. **Serves 4.**

Kery Mueller
Mother of Madison Mueller '12 and Caroline Mueller '15

To Serve: Garnish with lemon slices and parsley. You may add either toasted almonds or capers for a different flavor.

Scott Griffin's Steak Seasoning

3 1/2 teaspoons salt
2 teaspoons onion salt
1 teaspoon onion powder
1 teaspoon dried onion flakes
1 1/2 teaspoons garlic powder
1 teaspoon cracked pepper

1 teaspoon oregano
1 teaspoon thyme
1/2 teaspoon cumin seeds
1 teaspoon Beau Monde
   seasoning

Grind the salt, onion salt, onion powder, onion flakes, garlic powder, pepper, oregano, thyme, cumin seeds and Beau Monde seasoning in a spice grinder or food processor to a fine powder. Rub generously on both sides of steak and let stand for 1 hour before grilling. Store any unused rub an airtight container. **Makes enough for 2 large steaks.**

Scott Griffin
Father of Britni Griffin '12 and Chandler Griffin '16

To Serve: We have already made large batches
to keep on hand in our kitchens.

Boat Dock Steak Marinade

3/4 cup soy sauce
1/4 cup Worcestershire sauce
1/2 cup red wine vinegar
1/2 cup fresh lemon juice
2 garlic cloves, minced

2 tablespoons dry mustard
2 1/4 teaspoons kosher salt
1 tablespoon pepper
1 1/2 cups vegetable oil

Mix the soy sauce, Worcestershire sauce, vinegar, lemon juice, garlic, mustard, salt and pepper in a bowl. Stir in the oil. Pour over steaks in doubled sealable plastic bag. Seal tightly and turn to coat. Marinate in the refrigerator for 2 hours or longer. Remove the steaks and discard the marinade before grilling the steaks. **Makes enough for 2 large steaks.**

Luke Young '75

Blender Béarnaise Sauce

6 green onions, finely chopped
1 tablespoon unsalted butter
1 teaspoon dried tarragon
1/4 teaspoon salt
1/4 teaspoon dry mustard

1/4 cup wine vinegar
4 drops of Tabasco sauce
4 egg yolks
2 cups (4 sticks) unsalted
   butter, melted

Sauté the green onions in 1 tablespoon butter in a skillet until tender, do not let brown. Remove to a blender. Add the tarragon, salt, mustard, vinegar, Tabasco sauce and egg yolks. Process at medium speed for 2 minutes. Add 2 cups butter gradually, processing constantly at medium speed until blended. Remove to a bowl and chill. Allow to soften at room temperature before serving. **Serves 10 to 12.**

Pat Shoemaker Taliaferno
Founding Board of Heritage Hall Trustees
Mother of Katie Shoemaker Bates '72 and Patti Shoemaker '73

Easy Hollandaise Sauce

1/4 cup (1/2 stick) butter
1/4 cup light cream
1 tablespoon lemon juice,
   or to taste

2 egg yolks
1/2 teaspoon dry mustard
1/4 teaspoon salt
Dash of Tabasco sauce

Microwave the butter in a 4-cup glass measuring cup until melted. Stir in the cream. Add the lemon juice, egg yolks, mustard, salt and Tabasco sauce and mix well. Microwave on High for 30 seconds. Stir to mix well. Microwave on High until cooked to the desired consistency, stirring every 30 seconds. **Serves 4.**

Sydney Graves Carey '79

To Serve: *Pour over fresh asparagus, eggs benedict, grilled fish, or maybe just eat it with a spoon!*

Sweet Hot Mustard

1 (4-ounce) can dry mustard
1 cup malt vinegar
1 cup sugar
3 eggs, beaten

Combine the mustard and vinegar in a jar with a tight-fitting lid and shake well. Let stand for 8 to 10 hours. Combine the mustard mixture, sugar and eggs in the top of a double boiler and mix well. Cook over simmering water until very thick, stirring frequently. Remove to a bowl. Chill, covered, for 3 days or longer before using. May be stored in the refrigerator for up to 2 weeks. Use a small amount in Caesar salad dressing or deviled eggs. It is good on all kinds of sandwiches. **Makes 1 1/2 cups.**

Crosby Norville Harris '77
Mother of Helen Harris '09, Meridith Harris '10,
Mark Harris '13 and Joseph Harris '16

Blue Cheese Mustard Sauce

3/4 cup half-and-half
4 ounces blue cheese
1/4 cup whole grain mustard
2 tablespoons Sweet
Hot Mustard (above)

Minced garlic to taste
Salt and black pepper
 to taste
Cayenne pepper to taste

Mix the half-and-half, cheese, whole grain mustard, Sweet Hot Mustard, garlic, salt, black pepper and cayenne pepper in a saucepan. Cook over medium heat until the cheese is melted, stirring frequently. Serve over beef tenderloin or steak. **Makes 1 cup.**

Crosby Norville Harris '77
Mother of Helen Harris '09, Meridith Harris '10,
Mark Harris '13 and Joseph Harris '16

To Serve: Drizzle over steaks or serve with Brown Sugar Molasses Ham (page 93) and small buns.

Garlic Herb Aïoli

3/4 cup mayonnaise
1/3 cup sour cream
2 garlic cloves, grated
1/2 cup chopped parsley
1/4 teaspoon paprika
1 teaspoon lemon juice
1/4 cup chopped chives

Combine the mayonnaise, sour cream, garlic, parsley, paprika, lemon juice and chives in a bowl and mix well. Chill before serving. Great served with smoked salmon. **Serves 4.**

Paula Walker

Mother of Mark Walker '71, Lynn Walker Stonecipher '78 and Rob Walker '85
Grandmother of Callahan Walker '17 and Kate Walker '19

Jolly Red Relish

16 ounces fresh cranberries
2 apples, cored and finely chopped
Juice of 2 oranges
1 (8-ounce) can crushed pineapple
1 cup chopped pecans
1 1/2 cups sugar

Process the cranberries in a food processor until finely chopped. Remove to a bowl. Add the apples, orange juice, pineapple, pecans and sugar and mix well. Chill, covered, for 8 to 10 hours. **Makes 2 quarts.**

Lea Ann Patterson
Mother of Steven Patterson '03 and Samantha Patterson '07

To Serve: This is the perfect side to add color to your holiday plate!

Desserts

Desserts

Chocolate Crunch Praline
 Tower Cake
German Chocolate Cake
Me Mo's Chocolate Cake
Italian Cream Cake
Cranberry Cake with Hot
 Butter Sauce
Carrot Cake
Judy's Coconut Cake
Oatmeal Cake
Apple Cake
Grandmother Kolb's
 Banana Cake
Pumpkin Cake Roll
Ice Cream Roll with Citrus Sauce
Homemade Vanilla Ice Cream
Chocolate Sauce
Chocolate Soufflé with
 Caramel Sauce
Baked Fudge
Chocolate Éclair Dessert
Pear and Almond Dacquoise

Gingerbread with Lemon Sauce
Maple Pumpkin Cheesecake
Giant Toffee Cookies
Five Chip Cookies
Oatmeal Rock Cookies
Soft Molasses Cookies
Thumbprint Cookies
Butter Cookies
Mama Dorlac's Sugar Cookies
Russian Tea Cakes
Orange Cookies
Family's Favorite Cookie Bars
Butterscotch Bars
Lemon Bars
Pumpkin Pie Squares
Death-to-the-Diet Kahlúa
 Brownies
Anna Maude's Apple Pie
Favorite Cherry Pie
Coconut Chess Pie
Pumpkin Pecan Pie

Chocolate Crunch Praline Tower Cake

Cake
1/2 cup (1 stick) butter
2 ounces unsweetened chocolate
1 cup water
1 cup granulated sugar
1 cup packed brown sugar
1/2 cup chocolate syrup
1 1/2 teaspoons vanilla extract
3 extra-large eggs
1 cup quick-cooking oats
1 1/2 cups all-purpose flour
1 teaspoon baking soda
1/2 teaspoon salt

Filling
1/2 cup (1 stick) butter
1/4 cup whipping cream
1 cup packed brown sugar
3/4 cup chopped pecans
1 (16-ounce) jar hot fudge topping
2 cups heavy whipping cream
5 tablespoons confectioners' sugar
1/2 teaspoon vanilla extract

For the cake, combine the butter and chocolate in a saucepan. Cook over low heat until melted and smooth, stirring occasionally. Remove to a large mixing bowl and let cool slightly. Add the water, granulated sugar, brown sugar, chocolate syrup, vanilla, eggs and oats and beat well. Beat in the flour, baking soda and salt. Pour into three greased 9-inch cake pans. Bake at 350 degrees for 30 minutes.

For the filling, combine the butter, 1/4 cup cream, the brown sugar and pecans in a saucepan. Bring to a boil, stirring frequently. Cook for 2 to 3 minutes, stirring constantly. Pour evenly over the hot cakes in the pans. Place under the broiler until bubbly, watching carefully so that it doesn't burn. Remove to a wire rack and let cool. Remove the cakes carefully from the pans. Warm the hot fudge topping in the microwave or over a bowl of hot water until of a spreading consistency. Spread equally over the top of the cake layers. Beat 2 cups cream, the confectioners' sugar and vanilla in a bowl until stiff peaks form. Place one cake layer on a serving plate and spread with one-third of the whipped cream. Top with the next cake layer and spread with one-third of the whipped cream. Top with the remaining cake layer and spread with the remaining whipped cream. Garnish with chocolate curls and serve. **Serves 12.**

Tracey Swan
Mother of Brody Swan '15 and Hayley Swan '16

German Chocolate Cake

Cake
1 cup shortening
2 cups sugar
4 egg yolks, lightly beaten
2/3 cup buttermilk
2 1/2 cups sifted all-purpose flour
4 ounces German's sweet chocolate
1/2 cup boiling water
1 teaspoon baking soda
1/3 cup buttermilk
1 teaspoon salt

1 teaspoon vanilla extract
4 egg whites, stiffly beaten

Frosting
3 egg yolks, lightly beaten
1 cup sugar
2 cups whipping cream
1 tablespoon butter
1 (3-ounce) can shredded coconut
1 cup chopped pecans

For the cake, beat the shortening and sugar in a mixing bowl until light and fluffy. Beat in the egg yolks. Beat in 2/3 cup buttermilk alternately with the flour, beating well after each addition. Melt the chocolate in the boiling water in a bowl, stirring until smooth. Dissolve the baking soda in 1/3 cup buttermilk in a bowl. Stir into the chocolate mixture. Add the chocolate mixture to the batter and mix well. Stir in the salt and vanilla. Fold in the egg whites. Pour into three nonstick cake pans. Bake at 350 degrees for 30 to 35 minutes or until the cake tests done. Cool in the pans for 10 minutes. Remove to a wire rack to cool completely.

For the frosting, combine the egg yolks, sugar, cream, butter, coconut and pecans in the top of a double boiler. Cook over simmering water for 30 to 40 minutes or until thickened, stirring frequently. Remove from the heat and let cool until of a spreading consistency. Spread between the layers and over the top and side of the cooled cake. **Serves 12.**

Bettye Heldenbrand
Secretary to Mr. Malone, Former Headmaster of Heritage Hall
Mother of Cynthia Heldenbrand Freeman '75 and Mark Heldenbrand

Me Mo's Chocolate Cake

Cake	Frosting
1 1/2 cups vegetable oil	3/4 cup packed brown sugar
2 cups sugar	1/4 cup (1/2 stick) butter
2 eggs	1/4 cup milk
2 2/3 cups all-purpose flour	3 tablespoons baking cocoa
2 teaspoons baking soda	1 teaspoon vanilla extract
1/2 teaspoon salt	Confectioners' sugar
1 cup buttermilk	
1/2 cup baking cocoa	
1 teaspoon vanilla extract	
1 cup boiling water	

For the cake, beat the oil and sugar in a mixing bowl. Beat in the eggs. Add the flour, baking soda, salt, buttermilk, baking cocoa and vanilla and beat well. Stir in the boiling water. Pour into a greased and floured 9×13-inch baking pan. Bake at 350 degrees for 40 minutes or until the cake tests done. Remove to a wire rack to cool completely.

For the frosting, combine the brown sugar, butter, milk and baking cocoa in a saucepan. Bring to a boil, stirring frequently. Cook for 4 to 5 minutes, stirring frequently. Remove from the heat and let cool. Stir in the vanilla. Beat in enough confectioners' sugar to make of a spreading consistency. Spread over the cake and garnish with pecan pieces. **Serves 12.**

Deanya Britten
Grandmother of Adam Lewis '14 and Raylee Lewis '18

Italian Cream Cake

Cake
2¹/2 cups all-purpose flour
1 teaspoon baking soda
1 cup (2 sticks) butter or
  margarine, softened
2 cups sugar
5 egg yolks
1 cup milk
²/3 cup pecans,
  finely chopped
3 ounces flaked coconut
1 teaspoon vanilla extract

5 egg whites, at room
  temperature
¹/2 teaspoon cream of tartar
3 tablespoons light rum

Frosting
8 ounces cream cheese,
  softened
¹/2 cup (1 stick) butter, softened
1 (1-pound) package
  confectioners' sugar, sifted
1 cup chopped pecans
2 teaspoons vanilla extract

For the cake, grease and flour three 9-inch cake pans. Line the pans with waxed paper and grease the waxed paper. Mix the flour and baking soda together. Beat the butter in a mixing bowl until light and fluffy. Beat in the sugar at medium speed. Add the egg yolks one at a time, beating well after each addition. Beat in the dry ingredients alternately with the milk, beginning and ending with the dry ingredients. Stir in the pecans, coconut and vanilla. Beat the egg whites in a mixing bowl at high speed until foamy. Add the cream of tartar and beat until stiff. Fold the egg whites gently into the batter. Pour into the prepared cake pans. Bake at 350 degrees for 25 to 30 minutes or until a wooden pick inserted in the center comes out clean. Cool in the pans for 10 minutes. Remove to a wire rack and remove the waxed paper; cool completely. Sprinkle each cake layer with 1 tablespoon of the rum and let stand for 10 minutes.

For the frosting, beat the cream cheese and butter in a mixing bowl until smooth. Beat in the confectioners' sugar gradually until light and fluffy. Stir in the pecans and vanilla. Spread between the layers and over the top and side of the cake.
Serves 12.

Tina Dobson
Mother of Blake Dobson '15 and Lauren Dobson '16

Cranberry Cake with Hot Butter Sauce

Cake
2³/₄ cups all-purpose flour
1¹/₄ cups sugar
2 teaspoons baking powder
1 teaspoon baking soda
¹/₄ teaspoon salt
2 cups sour cream
¹/₂ cup milk
¹/₄ cup vegetable oil

¹/₂ teaspoon almond extract
2 eggs
12 ounces fresh cranberries

Sauce
2 cups sugar
1 cup (2 sticks) butter
1 cup half-and-half
1 teaspoon vanilla extract

For the cake, mix the flour, sugar, baking powder, baking soda and salt in a large bowl. Add the sour cream, milk, oil, almond extract, eggs and cranberries and mix well. Pour into a greased and floured 10×15-inch baking pan. Bake at 375 degrees for 30 to 40 minutes or until the cake tests done. Remove to a wire rack to cool. Cut into squares and place on serving plates. You may bake the cake in a 9×13-inch baking pan. Increase the baking time by 10 minutes.

For the sauce, combine the sugar, butter and half-and-half in a saucepan. Bring to a simmer, stirring occasionally. Simmer for 2 minutes, stirring frequently. Stir in the vanilla. Pour the hot sauce generously over the cake squares. **Serves 24.**

Jill Talley
Mother of Casey Talley '07, Cameron Talley '09 and Claire Talley '11

Carrot Cake

Cake
2 cups all-purpose flour
2 teaspoons baking powder
1 1/2 teaspoons baking soda
1 teaspoon salt
2 teaspoons cinnamon
4 eggs
2 cups sugar
1 1/2 cups corn oil
1 (8-ounce) can crushed pineapple
2 cups grated carrots (4 to 5 carrots)
1/2 cup pecans or black walnuts
1 (8-ounce) jar applesauce
1 cup raisins

Frosting
8 ounces cream cheese, softened
1/4 cup (1/2 stick) butter, softened
1 (1-pound) package confectioners' sugar
1 teaspoon vanilla extract

For the cake, mix the flour, baking powder, baking soda, salt and cinnamon together. Mix the eggs, sugar and corn oil in a bowl. Stir in the dry ingredients gradually and mix well. Stir in the pineapple, carrots, pecans, applesauce and raisins. Pour into a nonstick 10×14-inch baking pan. Bake at 350 degrees for 45 minutes or until the cake tests done. Remove to a wire rack.

For the frosting, beat the cream cheese, butter, confectioners' sugar and vanilla in a mixing bowl until smooth. Spread over the warm cake. **Serves 12.**

Penny Buxton
Grandmother of Stefan Dolese '14, Liesl Dolese '15 and
Renie Dolese '15

Judy's Coconut Cake

Cake
1 (2-layer) package white cake mix
3/4 cup cream of coconut
1/2 cup vegetable oil
3 eggs
1 cup sour cream

Frosting
8 ounces cream cheese, softened
9 tablespoons butter, softened
1 teaspoon vanilla extract
1 tablespoon cream of coconut
1 (1-pound) package confectioners' sugar
Shredded coconut

For the cake, beat the cake mix, cream of coconut, oil, eggs and sour cream in a mixing bowl until smooth. Pour into two greased and floured 9-inch cake pans. Bake at 350 degrees for 25 to 30 minutes; do not overbake. Cool in the pans for 10 minutes. Remove to a wire rack to cool completely.

For the frosting, beat the cream cheese, butter, vanilla, cream of coconut and confectioners' sugar in a mixing bowl until smooth. Spread between the layers and over the top and side of the cake, sprinkling shredded coconut between the layers and over the top. **Serves 12.**

Christy Knott Gordon '93 in loving memory of Judy Knott
Mother of Austin Gordon '14 and Gavin Gordon '16

To Serve: This cake is beautiful when decorated with fresh flowers.

Oatmeal Cake

Cake
1 1/2 cups boiling water
1 cup rolled oats
1/2 cup (1 stick) margarine, softened
1 cup packed brown sugar
1 cup granulated sugar
2 eggs
1 1/2 cups all-purpose flour
1 teaspoon baking soda
1/2 teaspoon salt
1 teaspoon cinnamon

Glaze
6 tablespoons butter, softened
1/2 cup packed brown sugar
1 cup shredded coconut
1/4 cup cream
1 teaspoon vanilla extract
1 cup pecans

For the cake, pour the boiling water over the oats in a bowl and let stand for 20 minutes. Combine the margarine, brown sugar, granulated sugar, eggs, flour, baking soda, salt and cinnamon in a mixing bowl and beat well. Stir in the oat mixture. Pour into a nonstick 9×13-inch baking pan. Bake at 325 degrees for 30 to 40 minutes or until the cake tests done.

For the glaze, combine the butter, brown sugar, coconut, cream, vanilla and pecans in a bowl and mix well. Spread over the hot cake. Broil for 3 minutes or until golden brown. Remove to a wire rack to cool. **Serves 15.**

Vicki Howard
Mother of Michael Howard '07 and Matthew Howard '11

Amy Crowley
Mother of Blake Crowley '14 and Paige Crowley '16

Apple Cake

Cake
2 cups sugar
2 eggs
1 cup vegetable oil
1 teaspoon vanilla extract
2 cups all-purpose flour
1 teaspoon baking soda
1 teaspoon salt
1 teaspoon cinnamon
3 cups diced peeled apples
1/2 cup chopped pecans

Sauce
1/2 cup (1 stick) butter
1/2 cup cream
1 cup sugar
1 teaspoon vanilla extract

For the cake, beat the sugar and eggs in a mixing bowl. Add the oil and vanilla and beat well. Mix the flour, baking soda, salt and cinnamon in a bowl. Add the apples and pecans and mix well. Stir into the batter. Pour into a greased and floured 9×13-inch baking pan. Bake at 350 degrees for 50 to 60 minutes or until the cake tests done. Remove to a wire rack to cool completely. The cake may be baked in two loaf pans. Adjust the baking time accordingly.

For the sauce, combine the butter, cream, sugar and vanilla in a saucepan. Bring to a boil, stirring frequently. Boil for 1 1/2 minutes, stirring constantly. Serve over the cake. **Serves 12.**

Nadine Carter
Grandmother of Katrina Larson '09 and Trevor Larson '08

To Serve: Serve with Homemade Vanilla Ice Cream (page 131).
You may bake the cake and freeze it.

Grandmother Kolb's Banana Cake

Cake
2 cups sifted cake flour
1 teaspoon baking soda
1/2 cup (1 stick) butter, softened
1 1/2 cups sugar
2 eggs
3 bananas, mashed
1/2 cup chopped pecans
1/4 cup buttermilk

Frosting
1/2 cup (1 stick) butter, softened
1 (1-pound) package confectioners' sugar
2 very ripe bananas, mashed
1/2 cup chopped pecans
1/2 teaspoon lemon juice

For the cake, sift the flour and baking soda together. Beat the butter and sugar in a mixing bowl until light and fluffy. Beat in the eggs. Stir in the bananas and pecans. Beat in the dry ingredients alternately with the buttermilk, beating well after each addition. Pour into two or three greased and floured cake pans. Bake at 325 degrees for 30 minutes or until the cake tests done. Cool in the pans for 10 minutes. Remove to a wire rack to cool completely. Chill in the freezer for 30 minutes before icing.

For the frosting, beat the butter and confectioners' sugar in a mixing bowl until the consistency of whipped cream. Stir in the bananas, pecans and lemon juice. Spread between the layers and over the top and side of the cold cake. Chill until the icing is firm. **Serves 12.**

Karen Kolb Flynn '72 and Kristy Kolb Jordan '74

Pumpkin Cake Roll

3/4 cup all-purpose flour
1 teaspoon baking powder
2 teaspoons cinnamon
1 teaspoon ginger
1/2 teaspoon nutmeg
1/2 teaspoon salt
3 eggs
1 cup granulated sugar
2/3 cup canned pumpkin pie filling
1 teaspoon lemon juice
1 cup finely chopped pecans
Confectioners' sugar for sprinkling
6 ounces cream cheese, softened
1/4 cup (1/2 stick) butter, softened
1 teaspoon vanilla extract
1 cup confectioners' sugar

Mix the flour, baking powder, cinnamon, ginger, nutmeg and salt together. Beat the eggs in a mixing bowl at high speed for 5 minutes. Beat in the granulated sugar gradually. Stir in the pie filling and lemon juice. Fold in the dry ingredients gradually. Spread into a greased and floured 10×15-inch baking pan. Sprinkle with the pecans, pressing lightly into the batter. Bake at 375 degrees for 15 minutes or until the cake tests done. Sprinkle a clean linen or cotton kitchen towel with confectioners' sugar. Invert the cake onto the towel. Roll the warm cake in the towel as for a jelly roll from the short side and place on a wire rack to cool. Beat the cream cheese, butter, vanilla and 1 cup confectioners' sugar in a bowl until smooth. Unroll the cooled cake carefully and remove the towel. Trim the outside end if it has hardened. Spread the cream cheese mixture evenly over the unrolled cake and reroll. Wrap the cake in foil and chill until serving time. Garnish with washed and dried greenery and mums for Thanksgiving or pine boughs and cranberries for Christmas. **Serves 10.**

Beth Wells
Mother of Courtney Wells '99 and Brenna Wells '02

Julie Gist
Aunt of Blake Crowley '14 and Paige Crowley '16

Ice Cream Roll with Citrus Sauce

Cake

1 cup all-purpose flour
1 teaspoon baking powder
1/2 teaspoon salt
3 eggs
1 cup granulated sugar
1/3 cup water
1 teaspoon vanilla extract
Confectioners' sugar for sprinkling
1 gallon vanilla ice cream, softened

Sauce

1 cup granulated sugar
1/4 teaspoon salt
2 tablespoons cornstarch
1 cup citrus punch
1/4 cup lemon juice
3/4 cup boiling water
1 tablespoon butter

For the cake, grease a 10×15-inch baking pan. Line the pan with foil or baking parchment and grease the foil. Mix the flour, baking powder and salt together. Beat the eggs in a mixing bowl until thick and pale yellow. Beat in the granulated sugar gradually. Beat in the water and vanilla at low speed. Beat in the dry ingredients slowly and beat just until smooth. Pour into the prepared pan. Bake at 375 degrees for 12 to 15 minutes or until the cake tests done. Loosen from the side of the pan with a sharp knife. Sprinkle a clean linen or cotton kitchen towel with confectioners' sugar. Invert the cake onto the towel. Remove the foil. Roll the warm cake in the towel as for a jelly roll from the short side and place on a wire rack to cool. Unroll the cooled cake carefully onto a sheet of foil and remove the towel. Spread the ice cream 1 inch thick evenly over the unrolled cake and reroll. Wrap the cake in foil and freeze until firm.

For the sauce, mix the sugar, salt and cornstarch in a saucepan. Stir in the punch, lemon juice and boiling water. Bring to a boil, stirring frequently. Boil for 1 minute, stirring frequently. Remove from the heat and stir in the butter. Serve warm over slices of the cake. **Serves 10.**

Irene Miller
Great-grandmother of Avery Niemann '15 and Ashton Niemann '18

To Learn: The sauce can be made well ahead of time and heated up as needed.

Homemade Vanilla Ice Cream

6 eggs	1 quart (4 cups) half-and-half
1 1/2 cups sugar	3 tablespoons vanilla extract
1 (14-ounce) can sweetened condensed milk	4 cups (about) milk

Beat the eggs in a mixing bowl until foamy. Beat in the sugar, condensed milk, half-and-half and vanilla. Pour into an ice cream freezer container and add the milk to the fill line. Freeze using the manufacturer's directions. Add 16 ounces frozen strawberries and 3 mashed bananas to the egg mixture to make strawberry banana ice cream. If you are concerned about using raw eggs, use eggs pasteurized in their shells, which are sold at some specialty food stores, or use an equivalent amount of pasteurized egg substitute. **Makes 1 gallon.**

Kelley Meacham
Mother of Connor Meacham '12, Morgan Meacham '16 and
Seth Meacham '18

To Serve: Great on a hot summer day with our
Homemade Chocolate Sauce (below).

Chocolate Sauce

1 cup sugar	1 teaspoon butter
2 tablespoons baking cocoa	1 teaspoon vanilla extract
1/4 cup light corn syrup	3 tablespoons evaporated milk
1/4 cup water	

Combine the sugar, baking cocoa, corn syrup and water in a saucepan. Bring to a full boil, stirring frequently. Remove from the heat. Stir in the butter, vanilla and evaporated milk. Let stand until cool. Store in an airtight container in the refrigerator. **Serves 8 to 10.**

Sarah Blackledge Brawley
Mother of Blair Brawley '20

Chocolate Soufflé with Caramel Sauce

Sauce
1/2 cup sugar
1/2 cup water
3/4 cup corn syrup
1 cup heavy cream, warmed
1 teaspoon vanilla extract

Soufflé
8 ounces bittersweet
   chocolate
1/2 cup (1 stick) butter
2 tablespoons heavy cream
4 egg yolks
7 egg whites
1/4 teaspoon cream of tartar
1/4 cup sugar
Sugar for dusting

For the sauce, mix the sugar, water and corn syrup in a saucepan. Bring to a boil without stirring. Boil, without stirring, until golden brown, watching closely so that the mixture doesn't burn. Remove from the heat and let cool slightly. Stir in the cream and vanilla. Serve or chill until serving time. Warm before serving.

For the soufflé, place the chocolate in the top of a double boiler over simmering water or in a heavy saucepan over low heat. Cook until the chocolate is melted, stirring occasionally. Remove from the heat and add the butter and cream. Stir until the butter is melted. Remove the mixture to a large bowl. Add the egg yolks one at a time, stirring well after each addition. Beat the egg whites with the cream of tartar in a mixing bowl until soft peaks form. Beat in the sugar slowly and beat until stiff. Fold the egg whites into the chocolate mixture. Butter six 1-cup ramekins and dust with sugar. Spoon the chocolate mixture into the prepared ramekins. Cover with plastic wrap and chill for up to 1 day or bake immediately. Arrange the ramekins in a shallow baking pan. Bake at 375 degrees for 20 minutes or until the tops are puffy and slightly cracked. Place the soufflés on individual serving plates and spoon the sauce over each soufflé. Serve immediately. **Serves 6.**

Lance Cook '98

Baked Fudge

5 eggs	1 cup (2 sticks) plus
2^1/4 cups sugar	2 tablespoons butter, melted
2/3 cup all-purpose flour	2 teaspoons vanilla extract
2/3 cup baking cocoa	

Beat the eggs in a bowl. Mix the sugar, flour and baking cocoa together. Add to the eggs and mix well. Mix the melted butter and vanilla in a bowl. Add to the cocoa mixture and mix well. Fill six to eight ramekins three-fourths full. Place the ramekins in a 9×13-inch baking dish. Add enough hot water to the baking dish to come one-quarter up the sides of the ramekins. Bake at 300 degrees for 45 minutes. Remove the ramekins to a wire rack to cool slightly. **Serves 6 to 8.**

Julie Keller
Mother of Kylee Keller '16, Chandler Keller '18 and Gray Keller '24

Chocolate Éclair Dessert

1 cup water	2 packets artificial sweetener
1/2 cup (1 stick) margarine	4 cups milk
1 cup all-purpose flour	8 ounces cream cheese,
4 eggs	softened
1 (6-ounce) package vanilla	9 ounces whipped topping
instant pudding mix	Chocolate syrup

Boil the water and margarine in a saucepan. Stir in the flour to form a ball. Let cool. Beat in the eggs one at a time. Spread into a greased 9×13-inch baking pan. Bake at 400 degrees for 30 minutes. Cool on a wire rack. Beat the pudding mix, artificial sweetener and milk in a bowl until smooth. Beat the cream cheese in a bowl until smooth. Stir in the pudding mixture. Spread over the cooled crust. Top with the whipped topping. Chill until serving time. Drizzle with chocolate syrup. **Serves 8 to 12.**

Joan Allen
Mother of Coach Kelly Allen
Grandmother of Matthew McLaughlin '15, Garrett McLaughlin '16
and Libby McLaughlin '19

Pear and Almond Dacquoise

Sauce
1 pint fresh raspberries
3 tablespoons sugar
1 tablespoon amaretto

Meringue
6 egg whites, at room temperature
1/2 teaspoon cream of tartar
1 1/4 cups superfine sugar

2/3 cup blanched almonds, ground

Filling
2 cups heavy whipping cream
1 to 2 tablespoons pear liqueur (optional)
2 tablespoons sugar
1 to 2 pears
1 tablespoon lemon juice
Confectioners' sugar for dusting

For the sauce, mix the raspberries, sugar and liqueur in a saucepan. Bring to a boil and cook until thickened, stirring frequently. Strain the sauce into a bowl.

For the meringue, line two baking sheets with baking parchment. Mark a 9-inch circle on the center of each piece of baking parchment. Beat the egg whites in a mixing bowl until foamy. Add the cream of tartar and beat at high speed until stiff but not dry. Add 2 tablespoons of the sugar and beat for 10 seconds. Fold in the remaining sugar and the almonds quickly with a rubber spatula. Divide the mixture evenly between the two baking sheets, spreading with a knife to fill the circles evenly. Bake at 300 degrees for 45 minutes. Reduce the oven temperature to 250 degrees and bake for 25 minutes longer or until the meringues are dry and very light brown. Remove the meringues and baking parchment to a wire rack and let cool for 15 minutes. Remove the meringues from the baking parchment carefully to a wire rack to cool completely.

For the filling, whip the cream in a mixing bowl. Beat in the liqueur and sugar. Peel and thinly slice the pears. Sprinkle the pear slices with the lemon juice. Place one meringue on a serving plate and arrange one-half of the pear slices over the top. Spread one-half of the whipped cream over the pears. Top with the remaining meringue. Arrange the remaining pear slices over the meringue and top with the remaining whipped cream. Spoon the sauce over the top and dust with confectioners' sugar. **Serves 8.**

Helen Swanson
Grandmother of Molly Remondino '14 and Annie Remondino '18

Gingerbread with Lemon Sauce

Gingerbread
1 cup all-purpose flour
1 teaspoon baking soda
$1/2$ teaspoon salt
1 teaspoon cinnamon
1 teaspoon ginger
$1/4$ cup ($1/2$ stick) butter, softened
$1/2$ cup sugar
1 egg, lightly beaten

$1/4$ cup molasses
$1/2$ cup buttermilk

Sauce
1 cup sugar
$1/2$ cup (1 stick) butter
$1/4$ cup water
1 egg, well beaten
$3/4$ teaspoon grated lemon zest
3 tablespoons lemon juice

For the gingerbread, mix the flour, baking soda, salt, cinnamon and ginger together. Beat the butter and sugar in a mixing bowl until light and fluffy. Beat in the egg. Beat in the molasses and buttermilk. Beat in the dry ingredients. Pour into a greased 8×8-inch baking pan. Bake at 350 degrees for 30 minutes or until the cake tests done. Remove to a wire rack.

For the sauce, combine the sugar, butter, water, egg, lemon zest and lemon juice in a saucepan. Bring to a boil, stirring constantly. Cook until thickened, stirring constantly. Serve over the warm gingerbread. **Serves 9.**

Wanda Brundrett (Mrs. Leyton)
Grandmother of Blake Crowley '14 and Paige Crowley '16

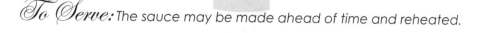

To Serve: The sauce may be made ahead of time and reheated.

Maple Pumpkin Cheesecake

Crust
1 1/4 cups graham
cracker crumbs
1/4 cup sugar
1/4 cup (1/2 stick) butter, melted

Filling
24 ounces cream cheese,
softened
1 (14-ounce) can sweetened
condensed milk

1 (15-ounce) can pumpkin
3 eggs, lightly beaten
1/4 cup maple syrup
1 1/2 teaspoons cinnamon
1 teaspoon nutmeg
4 teaspoons cornstarch
2 tablespoons water
2 tablespoons butter
1/2 cup maple syrup
1/2 cup raisins
1/2 cup chopped walnuts

For the crust, combine the graham cracker crumbs, sugar and butter in a bowl and mix well. Press over the bottom of a greased 9-inch springform pan.

For the filling, beat the cream cheese and condensed milk in a mixing bowl until smooth. Beat in the pumpkin. Add the eggs and beat just until combined. Stir in 1/4 cup maple syrup, the cinnamon and nutmeg. Pour into the prepared crust and place the springform pan on a baking sheet. Bake at 375 degrees for 70 to 75 minutes or until the center is barely set. Remove to a wire rack to cool for 10 minutes. Loosen from the side of the pan with a sharp knife and let cool for 1 hour. Place the cheesecake in the pan on a serving plate. Mix the cornstarch and water in a bowl until smooth. Melt the butter in a saucepan. Stir in the cornstarch mixture and 1/2 cup maple syrup. Bring to a boil, stirring constantly. Cook for 1 to 2 minutes or until thickened, stirring constantly. Remove from the heat and stir in the raisins and walnuts. Let cool to lukewarm. Spoon over the top of the cheesecake. Chill for 8 to 10 hours. Remove the side of the pan and serve. **Serves 12 to 14.**

Katherine Lagaly
Aunt of Avery Niemann '15 and Ashton Niemann '18

Giant Toffee Cookies

1/2 cup all-purpose flour
1 teaspoon baking powder
1/4 teaspoon salt
2 2/3 cups (16 ounces) semisweet chocolate chips
1/4 cup (1/2 stick) unsalted butter

1 3/4 cups packed brown sugar
4 eggs
1 tablespoon vanilla extract
1 package chocolate-covered toffee bits
1 cup walnuts, chopped

Mix the flour, baking powder and salt together. Combine the chocolate chips and butter in the top of a double boiler. Cook over simmering water until melted, stirring until smooth. Remove from the heat and let cool to lukewarm. Beat the brown sugar and eggs in a mixing bowl for 5 minutes or until thickened. Add the chocolate mixture and vanilla and beat well. Stir in the dry ingredients, toffee bits and walnuts. Chill for 1 hour or until firm. Drop by heaping spoonfuls 2 inches apart onto a baking parchment-lined cookie sheet. Bake at 350 degrees for 12 to 14 minutes or just until the tops are cracked and the cookies are still soft. Cool on the cookie sheet for 2 minutes. Remove the cookies and baking parchment to a wire rack to cool completely. Remove the cookies from the baking parchment when cool. **Makes 24 to 36.**

Genifer Ring
Mother of Matthew Ring '17, Blake Ring '19 and Samuel Ring '21
Wife of Robert Ring, Middle School English Teacher

To Learn: These may be made up to 2 days in advance.
Store in an airtight container.

Five Chip Cookies

2 cups all-purpose flour
1 cup rolled oats
2 teaspoons baking soda
1/2 teaspoon salt
1 cup (2 sticks) butter or
  margarine, softened
1 cup good-quality smooth or
  chunky peanut butter
1 cup granulated sugar
2/3 cup packed brown sugar
2 eggs

1 teaspoon vanilla extract
2/3 cup (4 ounces) milk
  chocolate chips
2/3 cup (4 ounces) semisweet
  chocolate chips
2/3 cup (4 ounces) peanut
  butter chips
2/3 cup (4 ounces) vanilla chips
2/3 cup (4 ounces)
  butterscotch chips

Mix the flour, oats, baking soda and salt together. Beat the butter, peanut butter, granulated sugar and brown sugar in a mixing bowl until light and fluffy. Beat in the eggs, vanilla and dry ingredients. Stir in the milk chocolate chips, semisweet chocolate chips, peanut butter chips, vanilla chips and butterscotch chips. Drop by spoonfuls onto nonstick cookie sheets. Bake at 350 degrees for 10 to 12 minutes. Cool on the cookie sheets for 2 minutes. Remove to a wire rack to cool completely. **Makes 48 to 60.**

Phyllis Cohlmia
Mother of Kim Cohlmia Musgrove '79, Jeff Cohlmia '82 and David Cohlmia '85

Oatmeal Rock Cookies

1 cup all-purpose flour
1/2 teaspoon baking soda
1/2 teaspoon salt
2 teaspoons cinnamon
1 teaspoon nutmeg
1/2 teaspoon cloves
1 cup (2 sticks) butter or
  margarine, softened

1 1/2 cups sugar
1/4 cup milk
2 eggs
1 teaspoon vanilla extract
4 1/2 cups rolled oats
1 cup chopped pecans
1 cup raisins

Mix the flour, baking soda, salt, cinnamon, nutmeg and cloves together. Beat the butter and sugar in a mixing bowl until light and fluffy.

Beat in the milk, eggs and vanilla. Add the dry ingredients and beat at low speed just until combined. Stir in the oats, pecans and raisins. Drop by spoonfuls onto a greased or baking parchment-lined cookie sheet. Bake at 350 degrees for 20 minutes. Cool on the cookie sheet for 2 minutes. Remove to a wire rack to cool completely. **Makes 72 to 96.**

Amy Crowley
Mother of Blake Crowley '14 and Paige Crowley '16

Soft Molasses Cookies

4 cups all-purpose flour
$1/2$ teaspoon salt
$2^1/4$ teaspoons baking powder
$2^1/4$ teaspoons cinnamon
$1^1/2$ teaspoons ginger
$1^1/2$ teaspoons cloves
$1/2$ cup shortening

$1/2$ cup (1 stick) margarine, softened
$1^1/2$ cups sugar
$1/2$ cup molasses
2 eggs, lightly beaten
Sugar

Whisk the flour, salt, baking powder, cinnamon, ginger and cloves in a bowl. Beat the shortening, margarine and sugar in a mixing bowl until light and fluffy. Beat in the molasses and eggs. Beat in the dry ingredients gradually. Shape into $1^1/2$-inch balls. Dip the tops of the balls into sugar and flatten with a glass dipped in sugar. Place $2^1/2$ inches apart on a greased cookie sheet. Bake at 350 degrees for 11 minutes; do not overbake. Cool on the cookie sheet for 2 minutes. Remove to a wire rack to cool completely. **Makes 36.**

In memory of Florinne Niemann
Grandmother of Avery Niemann '15 and Ashton Niemann '18

Thumbprint Cookies

1 (4-ounce) package vanilla
instant pudding mix
1 (10-ounce) package pie crust mix
2 tablespoons butter or margarine, melted
4 to 5 tablespoons cold water
Colored sprinkles
6 tablespoons butter or margarine, softened
1 egg white
Dash of salt
1 (1-pound) package confectioners' sugar
Food color (optional)
Milk

Stir the pudding mix and pie crust mix in a bowl. Add 2 tablespoons butter and 4 tablespoons of the water. Stir with a fork until the mixture forms a soft dough, adding the additional tablespoon of water if the dough is too dry. Shape into 1-inch balls. Roll in sprinkles. Place 1 inch apart on an ungreased cookie sheet. Make a deep indentation in each cookie with your thumb. Bake at 350 degrees for 15 minutes or until light brown. Cool on the cookie sheet for 2 minutes. Remove to a wire rack to cool completely. Beat 6 tablespoons butter, the egg white, salt and confectioners' sugar in a bowl until smooth. Stir in enough food color until of the desired tint. Thin with milk, if desired. Spoon into a decorator tube and pipe into the indentation on the cooled cookies. If you are concerned about using a raw egg white, use an egg white from an egg pasteurized in its shell, or use an equivalent amount of meringue powder and follow the package directions. **Makes 24 to 36.**

Kara Brown
Mother of Callan Brown '06 and Travis Brown '08

To Learn: Use the back of a melon baller to make
perfect "thumbprints" every time.

Butter Cookies

1 cup (2 sticks) butter or margarine, softened
2/3 cup granulated sugar
1 egg yolk
1 teaspoon vanilla extract or almond extract
1/4 teaspoon salt
2 1/3 cups all-purpose flour
Milk
1 cup confectioners' sugar
1/4 teaspoon vanilla extract or
almond extract (optional)
Food color

Beat the butter and granulated sugar in a mixing bowl until light and fluffy. Beat in the egg yolk, 1 teaspoon vanilla and the salt. Beat in the flour gradually. Roll 1/8 inch thick on a floured surface. Cut with cookie cutters. Place on an ungreased cookie sheet. Bake at 350 degrees for 8 to 10 minutes or until light brown. Cool on the cookie sheet for 2 minutes. Remove to a wire rack to cool completely. Stir enough milk into the confectioners' sugar in a bowl until of a spreading consistency. Stir in 1/4 teaspoon vanilla. Stir in enough food color until of the desired tint. Frost the cooled cookies. **Makes 24 to 36.**

Crystal Hardberger
Mother of Kate Hardberger '16 and Max Hardberger '19

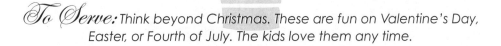

To Serve: Think beyond Christmas. These are fun on Valentine's Day, Easter, or Fourth of July. The kids love them any time.

Mama Dorlac's Sugar Cookies

2 cups (4 sticks) butter, softened
1 1/2 cups sugar
1 teaspoon vanilla extract

5 cups all-purpose flour
Additional sugar

Beat the butter, sugar and vanilla in a mixing bowl until light and fluffy. Beat in the flour; the dough will be dry. Shape into balls. Place on an ungreased cookie sheet. Flatten with a glass dipped in sugar. Bake at 400 degrees for 12 to 15 minutes; do not let brown. Cool on the cookie sheet for 2 minutes. Remove to a wire rack to cool completely. **Makes 48.**

Tracey Saunders
Mother of Trent Saunders '13 and Sayde Saunders '17

To Learn: This recipe originally came from the house mom at Oklahoma State University's Alpha Chi Omega house.

Russian Tea Cakes

1 cup (2 sticks) butter, softened
1/2 cup confectioners' sugar
1 teaspoon vanilla extract
2 1/4 cups all-purpose flour

1/4 teaspoon salt
3/4 cup finely chopped walnuts
Additional confectioners' sugar

Beat the butter, 1/2 cup confectioners' sugar and the vanilla in a mixing bowl until light and fluffy. Add the flour, salt and walnuts and stir until the dough holds together. Shape into 1-inch balls. Place 1 inch apart on an ungreased cookie sheet. Bake at 400 degrees for 10 to 12 minutes or until set but not brown. Cool on the cookie sheet for 2 minutes. Roll the warm cookies in confectioners' sugar and cool completely on a wire rack. Roll the cooked cookies in confectioners' sugar again before serving. **Makes 36.**

Melissa Gutwald
Mother of Matthew Gutwald '16

To Learn: It is very important to roll these cookies in the confectioners' sugar twice.

142

Orange Cookies

Cookies
1 cup (2 sticks) margarine, softened
1 1/2 cups sugar
1 cup sour cream
2 eggs
4 cups all-purpose flour
1 teaspoon baking soda
1 teaspoon baking powder
1/2 teaspoon salt
2/3 cup fresh orange juice
3 tablespoons grated orange zest

Icing
6 tablespoons butter, melted
1 tablespoon grated orange zest
3 cups confectioners' sugar
1/4 cup fresh orange juice

For the cookies, beat the margarine and sugar in a mixing bowl until light and fluffy. Beat in the sour cream and eggs. Beat in the flour, baking soda, baking powder, salt and orange juice. Stir in the orange zest. Drop by rounded teaspoonfuls onto an ungreased cookie sheet. Bake at 375 degrees for 8 to 11 minutes or until golden brown. Cool on the cookie sheet for 2 minutes. Remove to a wire rack.

For the icing, combine the butter, orange zest, confectioners' sugar and orange juice in a bowl and mix well. Drizzle over the hot cookies and let cool before serving. **Makes 72.**

Betty Daniels
Grandmother of Thea Daniels '01 and Isabel Daniels '05

To Learn: To freeze, layer with waxed paper. They freeze well and last several weeks. Remove from the freezer 1 hour before serving.

Family's Favorite Cookie Bars

1 (2-layer) package yellow cake mix
1/3 cup vegetable oil
2 eggs
2 cups (12 ounces) semisweet chocolate chips
1 cup (6 ounces) butterscotch chips
1 cup chopped chocolate-covered
toffee candy bar
1/2 cup (1 stick) butter
32 caramels
1 (14-ounce) can sweetened
condensed milk

Line a 9×13-inch baking pan with foil and coat the foil with nonstick cooking spray. Combine the cake mix, oil and eggs in a bowl. Mix with clean hands to a crumbly dough. Stir in the chocolate chips, butterscotch chips and chopped candy bar. Press half the dough over the bottom of the prepared pan. Bake at 350 degrees for 10 minutes. Combine the butter, caramels and condensed milk in a saucepan. Cook over low heat until the caramels are melted and the mixture is smooth, stirring frequently. Pour evenly over the hot baked crust. Crumble the remaining dough evenly over the caramel layer. Bake for 25 to 30 minutes longer. Remove from the baking pan by lifting the edges of the foil. Chill in the refrigerator until cool. Cut into small bars and store in an airtight container in the refrigerator. This recipe was handed down by my mother. You may add nuts for a variation. **Makes 24.**

Bonnie Clifton
Mother of Ross Clifton '12, Camille Clifton '13 and Bella Clifton '15

Butterscotch Bars

2¹/2 cups all-purpose flour
1 teaspoon baking powder
¹/2 teaspoon salt
1 cup (2 sticks) butter, softened
1³/4 cups packed brown sugar

1 tablespoon vanilla extract
2 eggs
1 cup (6 ounces)
   butterscotch chips

Mix the flour, baking powder and salt together. Beat the butter, brown sugar and vanilla in a mixing bowl until light and fluffy. Add the eggs one at a time, beating well after each addition. Beat in the dry ingredients slowly and beat just until combined. Spread the batter in a greased 9×13-inch baking pan. Sprinkle with the butterscotch chips. Bake at 350 degrees for 20 to 25 minutes. Remove to a wire rack to cool completely. Cut into bars when cool. **Makes 24.**

Stephanie Collison
Mother of Sydney Collison '14, Macy Collison '16 and Tori Collison '19

To Learn: Do not overcook. These should be slightly gooey.

Lemon Bars

1 cup (2 sticks) butter, softened
¹/2 cup confectioners' sugar
2 cups all-purpose flour
4 eggs
2 cups granulated sugar

Pinch of salt
6 tablespoons lemon juice
¹/4 cup all-purpose flour
Confectioners' sugar
   for dusting

Combine the butter, confectioners' sugar and 2 cups flour in a bowl and mix well. Press over the bottom of a greased 9×13-inch baking pan. Bake at 350 degrees for 20 minutes. Beat the eggs, granulated sugar, salt, lemon juice and ¹/4 cup flour in a mixing bowl. Pour over the hot baked crust. Bake for 25 minutes longer. Remove to a wire rack and dust with confectioners' sugar. Cut into bars when cool. **Makes 24.**

Wilma Mastell
Grandmother of Gavin Mastell '13, Baillie Miller '15 and Blake Miller '20

Pumpkin Pie Squares

1 (2-layer) package yellow cake mix
1/2 cup (1 stick) butter, melted
1 egg
1 (16-ounce) can pumpkin
1 tablespoon pumpkin pie spice
1/2 cup packed brown sugar
2 eggs
2/3 cup evaporated milk
1/4 cup granulated sugar
1 1/2 teaspoons cinnamon
3/4 cup chopped pecans (optional)
1/4 cup (1/2 stick) cold butter

Remove and reserve 1 cup of the cake mix. Combine the remaining cake mix, 1/2 cup butter and 1 egg in a bowl and mix well. Press over the bottom of a greased 9×13-inch baking pan. Combine the pumpkin, pumpkin pie spice, brown sugar, 2 eggs and the evaporated milk in a bowl and mix well. Pour evenly over the cake mix layer in the baking pan. Combine the 1 cup reserved cake mix, the granulated sugar, cinnamon and pecans in a bowl and mix well. Cut in 1/4 cup cold butter with a pastry blender or fork until crumbly. Sprinkle over the pumpkin layer. Bake at 425 degrees for 10 minutes. Reduce the oven temperature to 350 degrees and bake for 40 to 45 minutes longer. Remove to a wire rack. Cut into squares when cool. **Makes 24.**

Lynda West
Heritage Hall Library Media Director
1975–1981

To Serve: This definitely needs to be accompanied
with fresh whipped cream.

Death-to-the-Diet Kahlúa Brownies

16 ounces unsweetened chocolate
1 cup (2 sticks) butter or margarine
2 cups sugar
1 cup all-purpose flour
4 eggs, beaten
2 teaspoons Kahlúa
1 cup (6 ounces) semisweet chocolate chips
1 cup chopped pecans

Combine the unsweetened chocolate and butter in a heavy saucepan. Cook over low heat until melted and smooth, stirring constantly. Remove from the heat. Mix the sugar and flour in a bowl. Add the melted chocolate mixture, eggs and Kahlúa and mix well. Stir in the chocolate chips and pecans. Spread in a greased 9×13-inch baking pan. Bake at 325 degrees for 35 minutes or until the edge is firm and the center is soft. Remove to a wire rack to cool for 30 to 40 minutes before cutting in squares. Remove the squares to a serving plate and chill for 2 hours or longer before servings. **Makes 24.**

Sallie Reece
Grandmother of Brayden Richardson '10 and Logen Richardson '15

To Learn: Instead of Kahlúa, brandy or vanilla extract may be used.

Anna Maude's Apple Pie

6 to 7 apples
1/2 teaspoon cinnamon
1/2 teaspoon nutmeg
2 tablespoons cornstarch
1/3 cup cold water
1/2 cup sugar
2 teaspoons fresh lemon juice
1 (2-crust) pie pastry
2/3 cup sugar
2 tablespoons butter, cut into pieces

Peel the apples and place the peelings in a saucepan. Cover the peelings with more than 2 cups water. Cook until the peels are tender. Strain the liquid into a bowl and discard the peels. Measure 2 cups of the strained liquid into the saucepan and bring to a boil. Mix the cinnamon, nutmeg, cornstarch and 1/3 cup cold water in a bowl. Stir into the boiling apple liquid. Cook until clear, stirring constantly. Add 1/2 cup sugar and boil for 5 minutes, stirring frequently. Remove from the heat and stir in the lemon juice. Fit one pastry into a pie plate. Core and slice the apples. Mound the apples into the pie shell. Sprinkle with 2/3 cup sugar and dot with the butter. Cut slits in the remaining pastry and cut a 1-inch hole in the center. Fit the pastry over the apples and crimp the edge to seal. Bake at 400 degrees for 40 minutes. Pour the apple syrup mixture into the pie through the hole in the top crust. Bake for 5 minutes longer. Remove to a wire rack to cool. **Serves 8 to 10.**

Ellen Eisner
Mother of Grant Eisner '73
Grandmother of Blake Eisner '08

To Learn: Cooking the pie this amount of time will leave the apples *slightly crunchy, the way they were in Anna Maude's pies.*

Favorite Cherry Pie

2 cups sifted all-purpose flour
1 teaspoon salt
2/3 cup shortening
5 to 7 tablespoons cold water
2 cans pitted tart cherries
1 cup sugar

3 to 4 drops almond extract
2 tablespoons all-purpose flour
1 tablespoon butter,
   cut into pieces
Cinnamon-sugar

Sift 2 cups flour and salt into a stainless steel bowl that has been chilled in the freezer. Cut in the shortening with a pastry blender or fork until crumbly. Add the cold water 1 tablespoon at a time, tossing with a fork to mix after each addition. Shape the dough into two balls. Roll one ball into a 12-inch circle on a floured surface. Fit into a 9-inch pie plate. Combine the cherries, sugar, almond extract, 2 tablespoons flour and the butter in a bowl and mix well. Spoon into the pie shell. Roll the remaining dough ball into a 12-inch circle on a floured surface. Cut into 1 1/2-inch strips. Arrange lattice-fashion over the pie and crimp the edge to seal. Sprinkle the top with cinnamon-sugar. Bake at 400 degrees for 50 to 55 minutes. Remove to a wire rack to cool. **Serves 8.**

Lisa Sielert
Lower School Teacher

Coconut Chess Pie

3 eggs
1 teaspoon vanilla extract
1 1/2 cups sugar
1/4 cup (1/2 stick) butter, melted

1 cup milk
1 1/2 cups shredded coconut
1 unbaked (9-inch) pie shell

Beat the eggs in a mixing bowl until thick and pale yellow. Beat in the vanilla and sugar. Beat in the butter, milk and coconut. Pour into the pie shell. Bake at 350 degrees for 50 to 55 minutes. Remove to a wire rack to cool. **Serves 8.**

Deanna Allen
Grandmother of Natalie Braden '12

Pumpkin Pecan Pie

1 egg, lightly beaten
1 cup canned pumpkin
1/3 cup sugar
1 teaspoon pumpkin pie spice
1 unbaked (9-inch) pie shell
2/3 cup light corn syrup
2 eggs, lightly beaten
1/2 cup sugar
3 tablespoons butter, melted
1/2 teaspoon vanilla extract
1 cup pecan halves

Combine 1 egg, the pumpkin, 1/3 cup sugar and the pumpkin pie spice in a bowl and mix well. Spread in the pie shell. Combine the corn syrup, 2 eggs, 1/2 cup sugar, the butter and vanilla in a bowl and mix well. Stir in the pecans. Spoon over the pumpkin layer. Bake at 350 degrees for 50 minutes or until set. Remove to a wire rack to cool. **Serves 8.**

Kelly Everhart
Stepmother of Jessica Everhart '10

Restaurants

The Coach House Three Sisters Soup

Kam's Kookery Chicken Tortilla Soup

Kam's Kookery Fish Tacos

La Baguette Bistro Sea Bass à la Nage

Mahogany Prime Steakhouse French Onion Soup

Flip's Tortellini

The Mantle Wellington Trio

The Metro Wine Bar and Bistro Avocado Cucumber Soup

The Metro Wine Bar and Bistro Bread Pudding and Whiskey Sauce

Michael's Grill Curried Shrimp Soup

Michael's Grill Steamed Pears with Red Wine and Raspberries

Montford Inn Blue Corn Buttermilk Pancakes

Newton's Pumpkin Cranberry Muffins

North Fork Meat Loaf

Paseo Grill Cucumber Salad

Pearl's Famous Squash Rockefeller

Red Moon Café Roasted Corn and Poblano Chile Chowder

Redrock Canyon Grill Key Lime Pie

Red Prime Steak Green Chile Mac and Cheese

Virago Japanese Pork Dumplings

Virago Spicy Thai Lobster Shots

The Coach House Three Sisters Soup

6 tablespoons olive oil or clarified butter
1 cup diced red onion (1/4-inch dice)
1/2 cup diced poblano chile
2 cups fresh corn kernels (about 2 large ears of corn)
11/2 cups diced zucchini (about 1 zucchini)
1 teaspoon puréed garlic
1 teaspoon kosher salt
1/2 teaspoon freshly ground pepper
1/4 cup panko
1 tablespoon sherry vinegar
3 cups chicken stock or corn stock
11/2 cups pinto beans, cooked

Heat the olive oil in a saucepan over medium-high heat. Add the onion and chile and sauté just until the onion is translucent. Stir in the corn, zucchini, garlic, salt and pepper. Sauté for a few minutes. Stir in the bread crumbs gradually. Add the vinegar and stir to deglaze the pan. Stir in the stock and beans and reduce the heat. Simmer for 10 minutes. Remove 11/2 cups of soup to a blender and purée. Pour the puréed soup back into the saucepan and stir to mix. Simmer for 3 to 5 minutes and serve. **Serves 6.**

The Coach House
Oklahoma City, Oklahoma

To Learn: This recipe was featured at the 2007 Epcot Food & Wine Festival at Disney World, where Oklahoma was recognized. Chef Kurt Fleichfresser was asked to design food to showcase Oklahoma for the Centennial.

Kam's Kookery Chicken Tortilla Soup

1 poblano chile
1 pound boneless skinless chicken breasts, cut into 1/2-inch cubes
1 1/2 teaspoons cumin
1 1/2 teaspoons salt
1/2 teaspoon coriander
2 tablespoons olive oil
1 cup chopped onion
2 teaspoons chopped garlic
1 tablespoon tomato paste
1 cup fresh corn kernels, charred

6 cups chicken stock
1/4 cup chopped cilantro
2 teaspoons fresh lime juice
2 cups vegetable oil
6 stale corn tortillas, cut into 1/4-inch-wide strips
1 teaspoon Creole seasoning or Emeril's Essence (see below)
1/2 cup sour cream
1 teaspoon chopped chipotle chiles in adobo sauce
1 avocado, chopped

Place the poblano chile on a foil-lined baking sheet and broil until blackened, turning as needed. Remove the chile to a sealable plastic bag and seal the bag. Let stand for 5 minutes. Peel, seed and chop the chile. Season the chicken with the cumin, salt and coriander. Brown the chicken in hot olive oil in a saucepan over medium-high heat. Add the onion and garlic and sauté for 5 minutes. Add the tomato paste, chopped poblano chile and most of the corn, reserving some for garnish. Cook for 1 minute, stirring constantly. Add the stock; bring to a boil. Reduce the heat and simmer for 20 minutes. Stir in the cilantro and lime juice and remove from the heat. Cover and keep warm. Fry the tortilla strips in batches in 350-degree vegetable oil in a skillet or deep fryer for 1 1/2 to 2 minutes or until golden brown. Drain on paper towels. Season with the Creole seasoning. Mix the sour cream and chipotle chiles in a bowl. Ladle the soup into serving bowls. Top each with the sour cream mixture, fried tortilla strips, avocado and reserved corn.

The restaurant uses Emeril Lagasse's Essence available from www.emerils.com. To make a half recipe of Emeril's Essence, combine 2 1/2 tablespoons paprika, 2 tablespoons salt, 2 tablespoons garlic powder, 1 tablespoon onion powder, 1 tablespoon oregano, 1 tablespoon thyme, 1 tablespoon black pepper and 1 tablespoon cayenne pepper in a bowl. Mix well. **Serves 4 to 6.**

Kam's Kookery
Oklahoma City, Oklahoma

Kam's Kookery Fish Tacos

1¹/₂ cups all-purpose flour
Salt and pepper to taste
2 cups cornmeal
4 eggs
1 cup buttermilk
1¹/₂ pounds catfish, tilapia or
  cod fillets, cut into
  1¹/₂-inch cubes

Vegetable oil
Tortillas
Salsa
Guacamole
Chopped lettuce
Chopped tomatoes

Season the flour with salt and pepper in a shallow dish. Season the cornmeal with salt and pepper in a separate shallow dish. Whisk the eggs and buttermilk in a shallow bowl and season with salt and pepper. Season the fish with salt and pepper. Coat the fish in the flour, shaking off any excess. Coat the fish in the egg mixture and then coat well in the cornmeal. Heat 2 inches of oil in a heavy skillet or deep fryer to 350 degrees. Add the fish and cook until golden brown on all sides. Remove with a slotted spoon to a plate lined with paper towels. Keep warm in a 200-degree oven. Serve with warm tortillas, salsa, guacamole, lettuce and tomatoes. **Serves 4.**

Kam's Kookery
Oklahoma City, Oklahoma

La Baguette Bistro Sea Bass
à la Nage

1/4 cup olive oil
2 cups sliced shallots
2 cups diced Roma tomatoes
Salt and pepper to taste
2 cups white wine
3 cups fish stock or water
4 1/2 teaspoons herbes de Provence or
a combination of basil and thyme
Pinch of saffron
4 (6-ounce) sea bass fillets
8 jumbo shrimp, peeled
8 fresh or frozen mussels

To prepare the nage (an aromatic court-bouillon), heat the olive oil in a saucepan over medium-high heat. Add the shallots and sauté until beginning to brown. Stir in the tomatoes, salt and pepper and sauté until the tomatoes begin to release their juices. Stir in the wine and reduce the heat. Simmer for 10 minutes or until reduced by half. Stir in the stock, herbes de Provence, saffron, salt and pepper. Simmer until the saffron is released, turning the mixture a copper color.

To assemble, arrange the fish, shrimp and mussels in a shallow baking pan coated with oil. Pour the nage evenly over the seafood. Bake at 450 degrees for 15 minutes or until the seafood is cooked through. Serve with cooked rice or potatoes. For the best results, the nage can be made a day ahead and refrigerated. Reheat before adding to the seafood. **Serves 4.**

La Baguette Bistro
Oklahoma City, Oklahoma

Mahogany Prime Steakhouse French Onion Soup

1/4 cup (1/2 stick) margarine	1 teaspoon pepper
3 pounds yellow onions, thinly sliced	1/2 cup demi-glace
	4 cups water
1/4 cup beef base	Croutons
2 tablespoons Grand Marnier	Sliced baby Swiss cheese

Melt the margarine in a large saucepan. Add the onions and cook slowly just until they begin to caramelize, stirring occasionally. Stir in the beef base, liqueur and pepper. Stir in the demi-glace and water. Bring to a boil and reduce the heat. Simmer for 10 minutes, stirring occasionally. Ladle into ovenproof soup bowls and top with croutons and cheese. Arrange the bowls in a shallow baking pan. Broil until the cheese is melted and beginning to brown. **Serves 6.**

Mahogany Prime Steakhouse
Oklahoma City, Oklahoma

Flip's Tortellini

6 tablespoons marsala	1 cup heavy cream
1/2 (14-ounce) can quartered artichoke hearts, chopped	Salt and pepper to taste
2 tablespoons chopped scallions	2 cups tri-color tortellini, cooked and drained
1 tablespoon minced garlic	4 ounces grated Parmesan cheese

Cook the marsala, artichoke hearts, scallions and garlic in a skillet until reduced, stirring frequently. Stir in the cream, salt, pepper and tortellini. Cook for 1 1/2 to 2 minutes, stirring frequently. Add the cheese and cook until melted, stirring constantly. Pour into a large bowl. Garnish with parsley and serve. **Serves 4 to 6.**

Flip's
Oklahoma City, Oklahoma

The Mantle Wellington Trio

Beef Filling
2 pounds beef trimmings from tenderloin, rib-eye and strip steaks
Salt and pepper to taste
1 tablespoon minced garlic
1/2 cup (or less) red wine
1/4 cup (or less) olive oil

Mushroom Filling
3 tablespoons olive oil
1 1/2 pounds portobello mushroom caps
1 1/2 pounds button mushrooms

2 tablespoons minced garlic
Salt and pepper to taste
1/2 cup red wine

Shrimp Filling
2 tablespoons olive oil
1 pound shrimp, peeled and deveined
1 tablespoon minced garlic
1/4 cup minced shallots
Salt and pepper to taste
2/3 cup heavy whipping cream
1 tablespoon lobster base
Puff pastry sheets

For the beef filling, grill or broil the beef until cooked to the desired degree of doneness. Remove to a food processor container. Add the salt, pepper, garlic, wine and olive oil and pulse until finely chopped. Remove to a bowl and chill.

For the mushroom filling, heat the olive oil in a skillet. Add the portobello mushrooms, button mushrooms, garlic, salt and pepper and sauté until the mushrooms are tender. Stir in the wine and cook until almost all of the liquid has evaporated. Remove to a food processor and pulse until almost smooth. Remove to a bowl and chill.

For the shrimp filling, heat the olive oil in a skillet. Add the shrimp, garlic, shallots, salt and pepper and sauté just until the shrimp turn pink. Stir in the cream and lobster base. Cook until slightly thickened, stirring frequently. Remove to a food processor and pulse until finely chopped. Remove to a bowl and chill.

Lay the puff pastry sheets on a work surface. Cut with a cookie cutter. Spoon the beef filling onto the center of one-sixth of the pastry cut-outs. Repeat with the mushroom filling and shrimp filling. Top each with a pastry cut-out and crimp the edges with a fork to seal. Arrange the pastries on a baking sheet coated with nonstick cooking spray. Bake at 350 degrees for 15 to 20 minutes or until golden brown. **Makes 24 to 36.**

The Mantle
Oklahoma City, Oklahoma

The Metro Wine Bar and Bistro
Avocado Cucumber Soup

5 avocados, coarsely chopped
6 cucumbers, peeled, seeded and coarsely chopped
5 jalapeño chiles, seeded and coarsely chopped
3 tablespoons lemon juice
3 tablespoons lime juice
1 1/2 teaspoons puréed garlic
1 bunch green onions, coarsely chopped
1/4 cup chicken stock
3 cups sour cream
2 1/2 cups heavy cream
Salt to taste
1/4 teaspoon white pepper
3/4 teaspoon Tabasco sauce
1 1/2 teaspoons chopped fresh thyme
1 1/2 teaspoons puréed fresh basil
1 1/2 teaspoons Worcestershire sauce

Combine the avocados, cucumbers, jalapeño chiles, lemon juice, lime juice, garlic, green onions, stock, sour cream, cream, salt, pepper, Tabasco sauce, thyme, basil and Worcestershire sauce in a large bowl and purée with an immersion blender or purée in batches in a blender. Pour into a bowl and adjust the seasonings to taste. Chill the bowl of soup in a larger bowl partially filled with cold water and ice. Serve in chilled soup bowls and garnish each with a slice of cucumber and brunoise of red bell pepper (finely chopped red bell pepper cooked slowly in butter). **Serves 18 to 24.**

The Metro Wine Bar and Bistro
Oklahoma City, Oklahoma

The Metro Wine Bar and Bistro Bread Pudding and Whiskey Sauce

Pudding	Sauce
3 eggs, lightly beaten	9 eggs
4 cups milk	1 cup sugar
2 teaspoons vanilla extract	$1/2$ cup bourbon
$4^1/2$ cups granulated sugar	2 cups (4 sticks) butter, melted
1 cup packed brown sugar	
$1/4$ teaspoon cinnamon	
1 cup raisins	
2 loaves sliced Wonder white bread	
1 cup packed brown sugar	

For the pudding, combine the eggs, milk, vanilla, granulated sugar, 1 cup brown sugar, the cinnamon and raisins in a large bowl and mix well. Add the bread slices and gently knead with clean hands just until the liquid is evenly absorbed. Spoon into a greased 9×13-inch baking pan. Sprinkle 1 cup brown sugar evenly over the top and press gently into the bread mixture. Place the 9×13-inch baking pan in a larger baking pan. Add enough hot water to the larger pan to come halfway up the sides of the 9×13-inch baking pan. Bake at 350 degrees for $1^1/4$ hours or until puffed and golden brown.

For the sauce, beat the eggs and sugar in a mixing bowl until light and fluffy. Beat in the bourbon. Beat in the melted butter gradually. Chill until ready to serve. Slice the hot bread pudding. Place each serving in a deep plate or bowl. Pour the sauce generously over the top. If you are concerned about using raw eggs, use eggs pasteurized in their shells, which are sold at some specialty food stores, or use an equivalent amount of pasteurized egg substitute. **Serves 24.**

The Metro Wine Bar & Bistro
Oklahoma City, Oklahoma

Michael's Grill Curried Shrimp Soup

1 1/2 cups finely chopped onions
1/4 cup (1/2 stick) butter
1 tablespoon minced garlic
8 cups chicken stock
2 cups heavy cream

1 cup coconut milk
1/4 cup all-purpose flour
4 1/2 teaspoons curry powder
1 pound chopped deveined peeled fresh shrimp

Sauté the onions in the butter in a saucepan until tender. Add the garlic and sauté for 1 minute. Stir in the stock, cream and coconut milk. Simmer for 20 minutes. Whisk in the flour. Whisk in the curry powder. Adjust the seasonings to taste. Stir in the shrimp. Cook for 3 minutes or until the shrimp turn pink. Serve immediately. **Serves 8 to 10.**

Michael's Grill
Oklahoma City, Oklahoma

Michael's Grill Steamed Pears with Red Wine and Raspberries

1 1/4 cups dry red wine
1/4 cup sugar
Grated zest of 1 orange

4 firm Anjou pears, peeled, cut into halves and cored
1 pint raspberries

Combine the wine, sugar and orange zest in a large bowl. Stir until the sugar is dissolved. Arrange the pears, cut side down in a steamer basket over simmering water. Steam for 5 minutes. Remove the pears to the wine mixture and gently stir in the raspberries. Let stand until room temperature. Serve at room temperature or chilled. **Serves 8.**

Michael's Grill
Oklahoma City, Oklahoma

Montford Inn Blue Corn Buttermilk Pancakes

1/2 cup all-purpose flour
1/4 cup blue cornmeal
1 teaspoon baking soda
1/2 teaspoon salt
1 cup buttermilk
1 egg, at room temperature
3 tablespoons butter, melted

Mix the flour, cornmeal, baking soda and salt together. Stir the buttermilk, egg and butter in a bowl until smooth. Add the dry ingredients and stir just until moistened; lumps will remain. Pour 1/4 cup at a time onto a hot lightly greased griddle. Cook until bubbles appear on the surface and the underside is golden brown. Turn the pancake and cook until golden brown. Serve with your favorite syrup. **Serves 4.**

William Murray '85
Montford Inn Bed and Breakfast
Norman, Oklahoma

Newton's Pumpkin Cranberry Muffins

Apple Butter
2 cups applesauce
5 tablespoons sugar
1 cinnamon stick
2 teaspoons cinnamon
1 teaspoon allspice
1 teaspoon cloves

Muffins
2¹/₃ cups all-purpose flour
1 teaspoon baking powder
1 teaspoon baking soda
1 teaspoon salt

1 tablespoon cinnamon
1 teaspoon nutmeg
1 teaspoon allspice
1 teaspoon cloves
2 cups canned pumpkin
2 cups sugar
3 eggs
2/3 cup vegetable oil
2/3 cup buttermilk
1 tablespoon vanilla extract
1 cup sweetened dried
   cranberries
1 cup pecans, chopped

For the apple butter, mix the applesauce, sugar, cinnamon stick, cinnamon, allspice and cloves in a saucepan. Cook over medium-low heat until the mixture boils, stirring frequently. Remove and discard the cinnamon stick. Spoon into a bowl and chill until cool.

For the muffins, mix the flour, baking powder, baking soda, salt, cinnamon, nutmeg, allspice and cloves together. Beat the pumpkin, sugar, eggs, oil, buttermilk and vanilla in a mixing bowl at low speed. Add the dry ingredients and beat just until combined. Fold in the cranberries and pecans. Fill nonstick muffin cups two-thirds full. Bake at 375 degrees for 18 minutes or until a wooden pick inserted in the center comes out clean. Remove to a wire rack and let cool before removing from the muffin cups. Serve with the apple butter. **Makes 18 to 24.**

Newton's
Oklahoma City, Oklahoma

North Fork Meat Loaf

1 yellow onion, chopped
1 red bell pepper, chopped
1 cup chopped celery
1 ($1/2$-ounce) package fresh thyme
1 ($1/2$-ounce) package fresh sage
2 tablespoons chopped parsley
1 tablespoon chopped garlic
3 pounds ground beef
1 pound ground pork
1 pound ground veal
1 pound ground turkey
4 eggs
1 cup bread crumbs
1 cup veal stock
12 slices good-quality bacon

Pulse the onion, bell pepper, celery, thyme, sage, parsley and garlic in a food processor until finely chopped. Remove to a large bowl. Add the beef, pork, veal, turkey, eggs, bread crumbs and stock and mix well. Shape into a 4×12-inch loaf and wrap the bacon slices around the entire loaf. Place the meat loaf in a shallow baking pan. Bake at 350 degrees for 45 minutes or until cooked through. Let stand for 15 minutes before slicing. **Serves 28.**

North Fork
Oklahoma City, Oklahoma

Paseo Grill Cucumber Salad

4 cucumbers, peeled and
thinly sliced
3 tablespoons kosher salt
4 large jalapeño chiles, seeded
and thinly sliced
1 cup minced red onion

2 teaspoons herbes de
Provence
2 teaspoons mixed
peppercorns, ground
1/2 cup white vinegar

Toss the cucumbers and salt in a bowl. Let stand for 10 minutes. Add the jalapeño chiles, onion, herbes de Provence, peppercorns and vinegar and toss to combine. **Serves 10 to 12.**

Paseo Grill
Oklahoma City, Oklahoma

Pearl's Famous Squash Rockefeller

4 small yellow squash
1 cup (2 sticks) margarine,
melted
2 cups dry bread crumbs
1 1/2 teaspoons
granulated garlic
1 tablespoon anisette liqueur

1/4 cup (1 ounce) grated
Parmesan cheese
16 ounces frozen spinach,
thawed and drained
2 tablespoons chopped scallions
1/2 cup hollandaise sauce
(optional)

Cook the squash in a saucepan of boiling water just until tender; drain. Cut the squash into halves and scoop out the seeds and pulp, leaving a 1/4-inch shell. Chop the squash pulp with seeds. Combine the squash pulp, margarine, bread crumbs, garlic, liqueur, cheese, spinach and scallions in a bowl and mix well. Fill the squash shells with the spinach mixture and arrange on a baking sheet. Bake at 350 degrees for 20 minutes or until heated through. Serve topped with the hollandaise sauce. You may microwave the filled squash 1 to 2 minutes instead of baking in the oven. **Serves 8.**

Pearl's
Oklahoma City, Oklahoma

Red Moon Café Roasted Corn and Poblano Chile Chowder

2 tablespoons vegetable oil
2 poblano chiles, roasted, seeded and diced
1 1/2 cups diced yellow onions
1 teaspoon chopped garlic
2 cups vegetable broth
2 cups corn kernels, roasted
2 teaspoons kosher salt
1 teaspoon cayenne pepper
2 cups corn kernels, roasted
1 cup vegetable broth
1 cup milk
1 1/2 cups diced seeded tomatoes
1/2 cup cilantro, chopped

Heat the oil in a saucepan over medium heat. Add the chiles, onions and garlic and sauté until the onions are translucent. Stir in 2 cups broth, 2 cups corn, the salt and cayenne pepper. Simmer for 10 minutes. Purée 2 cups corn, 1 cup broth and the milk in a blender and add to the saucepan. Stir in the tomatoes. Simmer for 20 to 30 minutes. Stir in the cilantro and serve immediately. Garnish with crumbled feta cheese. **Serves 8 to 10.**

Red Moon Café
Oklahoma City, Oklahoma

166

Redrock Canyon Grill
Key Lime Pie

1 1/2 to 2 sleeves graham crackers, crushed
1 cup walnuts, finely chopped
1 cup pecans, finely chopped
2 tablespoons sugar
1/4 teaspoon cinnamon
1 to 3 tablespoons butter, melted
6 egg yolks
Grated zest of 8 key limes
2 (14-ounce) cans sweetened condensed milk
1 cup minus 2 tablespoons fresh key lime juice
Whipped cream

Combine the graham cracker crumbs, walnuts, pecans, sugar and cinnamon in a bowl and mix well. Stir in enough butter until the mixture comes together. Press over the bottom and up the side of a 10 1/2-inch pie plate. Bake at 325 degrees for 10 minutes. Remove to a wire rack to cool for 30 minutes. Combine the egg yolks and lime zest in a bowl and mix well. Add the condensed milk and lime juice and mix well. Pour into the warm pie shell. Bake at 325 degrees for 18 to 22 minutes. Remove to a wire rack to cool for 20 minutes. Chill for 8 to 10 hours. Serve topped with whipped cream. **Serves 8.**

Redrock Canyon Grill
Oklahoma City, Oklahoma

Red Prime Steak Green Chile Mac and Cheese

6 tablespoons heavy cream
2 ounces Gruyère cheese, shredded
1 ounce Monterey Jack cheese, shredded
1/2 ounce diced roasted poblano chile
4 1/2 teaspoons roasted poblano chile purée
Salt and pepper to taste
5 ounces rigatoni, cooked and drained
1 tablespoon toasted bread crumbs

Combine the cream, Gruyère cheese, Monterey Jack cheese, diced poblano chile and poblano chile purée in a saucepan. Bring to a gentle simmer, stirring constantly. Season with salt and pepper. Stir in the pasta and cook for 1 minute or until the sauce has thickened, stirring constantly. Remove to a serving bowl and top with the bread crumbs. **Serves 1.**

Red Prime Steak
Oklahoma City, Oklahoma

Virago Japanese Pork Dumplings

Sauce
1 part soy sauce
2 parts water
1 part rice wine vinegar
Thinly sliced scallions
(green part only)

Dumplings
8 ounces ground pork
4 slices unsmoked bacon or
pancetta, finely chopped
1 (1-inch) piece fresh ginger,
peeled and grated
4 scallions, thinly sliced
(green part only)

Pinch of Chinese five-spice
powder
1/4 teaspoon dark sesame oil
1/2 (8-ounce)can water
chestnuts, drained and
finely chopped
1 teaspoon sugar
1 teaspoon Asian chile sauce
1 egg white
Salt and pepper to taste
1 package round gyoza
wrappers, thawed
1 egg yolk
2 tablespoons water
Cornstarch
Vegetable oil

For the sauce, mix the soy sauce, water, vinegar and scallions in a bowl.

For the dumplings, combine the pork, bacon, ginger, scallions, five-spice powder, sesame oil, water chestnuts, sugar, chile sauce, egg white, salt and pepper in a bowl and mix well. Chill for 1 hour. Separate the wrappers on a work surface. Spoon a small amount of the pork mixture onto the center of each wrapper. Mix the egg yolk and water in a bowl. Brush the edges of the wrappers lightly with the egg mixture. Fold over the wrappers to make a crescent shape and crimp the edges to seal. Arrange the dumplings on a cornstarch-dusted plate, making sure the dumplings are not touching. Chill, covered, until ready to cook. Bring a large saucepan of water to a boil and add the dumplings. Cook for 5 minutes or until cooked through. Drain and shake dry. Heat a small amount of oil in a skillet. Add the dumplings and cook until golden brown on one side. Serve with thinly sliced cabbage and the sauce. **Makes 20 to 24.**

Clay Greenberg '85
Virago
Nashville, Tennessee

Virago Spicy Thai Lobster Shots

1 (14-ounce) can coconut milk
3¹/₂ tablespoons water
1 (2-inch) piece fresh ginger, peeled and chopped
4 garlic cloves, chopped
2 tablespoons sambal (chile paste)
¹/₂ teaspoon paprika (optional)
2 stalks of fresh lemon grass, trimmed and chopped
1¹/₂ tablespoons fish sauce
2 tablespoons sugar
4 fresh or frozen kaffir lime leaves
1 (2-inch) piece fresh or frozen galangal root,
peeled and chopped (optional)
1¹/₂ teaspoons fresh lime juice
Vegetable oil or canola oil
1 (8- to 10-ounce) lobster tail, cut into ¹/₂-inch pieces
Chopped cilantro

Combine the coconut milk, water, ginger, garlic, sambal, paprika, lemon grass, fish sauce, sugar, lime leaves, galangal and lime juice in a saucepan. Bring to a simmer and cook for at least 30 minutes, stirring occasionally. Pour through a fine mesh strainer into a saucepan and keep warm. Discard the solids. Heat an 8- to 10-inch skillet over medium-high heat. Add a small amount of oil to the skillet and heat for a few seconds. Add the lobster pieces, no more than twelve at a time, and sear for a few seconds on each side or until the lobster meat is opaque. Remove the lobster pieces with tongs to a plate and keep warm while cooking the remaining lobster. Return all the lobster to the pan and add the coconut mixture. Cook over high heat for 30 seconds and stir in chopped cilantro. Spoon one lobster piece into each sake cup and fill with the broth. Serve immediately. **Serves 16.**

Clay Greenberg '85
Virago
Nashville, Tennessee

Index

TO LEARN, TO LEAD... *To Serve*

ORDER INFORMATION

Heritage Hall
1800 NW 122nd Street
Oklahoma City, Oklahoma 73120
405-749-3001
www.heritagehall.com